It's
SUPPOSED
To Be
Impossible

ISBN 979-8-58161-468-6

Published by The Desire of the Nations, P.O. Box 1255, Rohnert Park, CA 94927

Dedicated to promoting the physical & spiritual welfare of nations, by working to surface the treasure in the hearts of the people.

Printed in the United States of America.

It's
SUPPOSED
To Be
Impossible

The Journey of Believing God
for All That He Has for You

Kevin Shipp

CONTENTS

ACKNOWLEDGEMENTS

To my beautiful and amazing wife, thank you for championing our vision and for being my best friend and my love. You are a tailor-made gift of God to my life.

To my kids for being the best kids in the world and for being willing to allow daddy to take time to pursue the desires of my heart. I love you to no end.

To Aunt Sandra Lund, Ann Telderer, Ashley Schrock, and Joy Schrock-Zipper, thank you so much for your expertise in your specific areas and for allowing me to tap into the wealth of your talents.

To my parents-in-love, Dave and Jan Kroll, and to my pastors Caleb and Rachel Klinge, thank you so much for your invaluable inspiration. You are priceless assets to our lives.

Lastly, to my parents… there are just no words. There is no way to articulate what you've done for me. I love you forever and ever!

Most of all, to our Lord and Savior, Jesus Christ; all honor, all glory, all blessing, majesty, and power, to you now, and forever and ever! Thank you for giving your life so that we can know you. We love you Lord Jesus.

CHAPTER 1
Let's Go!

Have you ever watched a movie that starts with the ending? One of my favorite movies, a spy movie, does that. It could be considered an oldie but goodie. As the movie unfolds there are bits and pieces of the story that are revealed along the way, with suspense, thrill, and some dramatic scenes, until the end, when there is the ultimate reveal. The "who dunnit?" That's the type of journey my family has been on over the last number of years. Our journey of following Jesus. My family consists of myself, Kevin; my wife, Robin; my son, Aiden; and my daughter, Kaeya.

For us, Jesus continually gives us glimpses of how amazing He is. You ask, "Well, what does that look like?" For the purposes of this story, the never-ending and constant revelation of His goodness and His glory, keeping us in a state of awe, is similar to a movie that begins with the ending. From reading the Bible and believing, we know the account of His love and character. Now, let's go back to the beginning of our experience with Him.

I grew up going to church consistently every Sunday through

my childhood, not by choice but because my parents brought me to church. I can't calculate the gratitude in my heart for that now, but it didn't start off that way. I didn't like church as a kid. Along with other kids my age, I sat on the back row often, not paying attention to what was going on in the service but laughing at whatever we could find entertaining. I would rather have been at home watching sports. So, I sat week after week, not realizing the reach that was being extended toward my indifferent heart by Jesus' love. I was pretty resistant then.

My wife, on the other hand, opened her heart to Jesus when she was six years old and grew up in an environment where miracles were normal. The opening of eyes of those born blind, opening of ears and healing of those born deaf/mute, etc. There were great things happening in my church experience, but I wasn't easily influenced. I was, and some might say I still am, more resistant to surrender than she is. The good thing is, God is persuasive. His kindness changes the heart, as the Bible says in the Epistle to the Romans, chapter 2:

> **4** *Do the riches of his extraordinary kindness make you take him for granted and despise him? Haven't you experienced how kind and understanding he has been to you? Don't mistake his tolerance for acceptance. Do you realize that all the wealth of his extravagant kindness is meant to melt your heart and lead you into repentance?*

Jesus eventually won my heart, but it was a couple of decades later. Because of the wonderful parents I had and the awareness of Jesus' reality, though, I didn't really want relationship with Him, I ended up with a childhood that was great on the outside. I have found, however, that there is no life better than a life with a heart being open to and intimately connected to Jesus. Part of the goal in our organization is to see children have an experience, unlike my resistant one, of the fullness of all God intends for them from childhood forward.

Going back to the analogy of a movie, there is often the question of "who dunnit?" Who committed the ultimate mysterious deed? Well, if it could be said this way, I've been watching this movie for a good amount of time now, and I can tell you that Jesus is the "who." The trail of evidence of His goodness is leading us further into greater levels of awareness of how much good He's done and continues to do. Desire of Nations is our organization, and we've been in love with Jesus and passionate about knowing Him in an ever-growing intimacy and also to see His love fill the hearts of everyone we know.

Family.

CHAPTER 2
The Goodness of God

This is an example of how He reveals His love. I was on a trip to Kenya, Africa, once and had the opportunity to speak before more people than I ever had before. This was an outdoor open-air meeting, and I was kind of nervous. I began talking to the Lord about it, and He told me to call my wife and tell her how I was feeling. She was back home in California with our son. When I reached her, I told her what was going on in my heart; and like the amazing wife that she is, she encouraged me. She also said, "I don't know what this is, but my ear has been stuffed all day, and I feel as though the Lord wants to heal someone's deaf ear." When she said this, I knew it was from God. After our conversation, I began to pray and ask the Lord about it, and He spoke to me that it was someone's left ear and it had been that way for a long time. So in this meeting, as it was my turn to share, I declared, "There is someone on these grounds that is deaf in your left ear, and Jesus wants to heal you." In short, there was a 9-year old boy who was born deaf in his left ear, whose mom testified she had tried several medical interventions, all to no avail. When Jesus touched him, he was completely healed.

These are the things our Jesus does. When these things happen, reminding us of the true kingdom of God, it leads us to hope like a child who has no care for where his next meal is coming from or whether the bills will be paid, going through life with expectancy of all that his or her imagination can grasp. This is the appropriate place for the mind of the child. A child of a king should dream with an even greater capacity. A child of the King of kings should dream with no limit. Jesus is the ultimate child. The ultimate child of God. He is also the Father of Eternity. As it says of Him in the Bible, in the book of Isaiah, chapter 9:

> **6** *A child has been born for us;*
> *a son has been given to us.*
> *The responsibility of complete dominion*
> *will rest on his shoulders, and his name will be:*
> *The Wonderful One!*
> *The Extraordinary Strategist!*
> *The Mighty God!*
> *The Father of Eternity!*
> *The Prince of Peace!*

Jesus revealed the heart of the Father, yet He received from His Father like a child. An example of Jesus as the amazing only begotten child of the King is found in the Gospel of Matthew, chapter 3:

> **1-2** *It was at this time that John the Baptizer began to preach in the desert of Judah. His message was this: "The realm of heaven's kingdom is about to appear—so you'd better keep turning away from*

evil and turn back to God!"

When I was growing up, I used to think this verse meant that we needed to get our act together or we were going to be in trouble. But the Lord has since shown me differently concerning His heart. The proclamation of necessity to turn away from evil was not limited to a mere punitive warning but, I believe more importantly, it was from a stewardship standpoint. In many verses, the Bible speaks of how God wants to endow us with His kingdom. The below verses show this.

> **Matthew 5:3** *"What wealth is offered to you when you feel your spiritual poverty! For there is no charge to enter the realm of heaven's kingdom.*

> **Matthew 11:12** *From the moment John stepped onto the scene until now, the realm of heaven's kingdom is bursting forth, and passionate people have taken hold of its power.*

> **Luke 12:32** *So don't ever be afraid, dearest friends! Your loving Father joyously gives you his kingdom realm with all its promises!*

Clearly, the Lord wants the kingdom to be given to his people to be a part of His loving reign. He says that to prepare to experience His kingdom and all that it is, we need to do something that the King James version of the Bible states in the Gospel of Matthew, chapter 3, verse 1, as "Repent". The definition of repent is "to think differently or change one's mind." Why is repenting necessary? Because if one is to receive the kingdom of God, He wants them to think like the King.

Jesus, being the King of kings, defines what a kingdom mindset looks like. As a King who had everything in His kingdom at His disposal, He thought from the perspective of Heaven's resources. When it was time to feed five thousand men plus women and children, Jesus told 12 men to feed them all with one boy's lunch.

> **Matthew 14:14** *So when Jesus landed he had a huge crowd waiting for him. Seeing so many people, his heart was deeply moved with compassion toward them, so he healed all the sick who were in the crowd.* **15** *Later that afternoon the disciples came to Jesus and said, "It's going to be dark soon and the people are hungry, but there's nothing to eat here in this desolate place. You should send the crowds away to the nearby villages to buy themselves some food."* **16** *"They don't need to leave," Jesus responded. "You can give them something to eat."* **17** *They answered, "But all we have is five barley loaves and two fish."* **18** *"Let me have them," Jesus replied.* **19** *Then he had everyone sit down on the grass as he took the five loaves and two fish. He looked up into heaven, gave thanks to God, and broke the bread into pieces. He then gave it to his disciples, who in turn gave it to the crowds.* **20** *And everyone ate until they were satisfied, for the food was multiplied in front of their eyes! They picked up the leftovers and filled up twelve baskets full!* **21** *There were about five thousand men who were fed, in addition to many women and children!*

Jesus' mindset was always that of abundance. He functioned from a mindset that God would supply all His needs according to His abundant riches of glory, which the Apostle Paul later wrote in the Epistle to the Philippians, chapter 4:

> **19** *I am convinced that my God will fully satisfy every need you have, for I have seen the abundant riches of glory revealed to me through the Anointed One, Jesus Christ!*

In the Gospel of John, chapter 6, this gospel's account of Jesus feeding the multitude says at the beginning part of the passage that Jesus knew what He would do. Because He knew what the Father's will was, He knew the resources to supply the need were completely available to Him; and this was so evident that the people ate as much as they would, and there were even leftovers! That is one example of the abundant life Jesus lived.

> **John 10:10** *A thief has only one thing in mind—he wants to steal, slaughter, and destroy. But I have come to give you everything in abundance, more than you expect—life in its fullness until you overflow!*

One can often think of how the "abundant life" that Jesus speaks of means that one's bills are paid and that one is completely healthy, and their family is saved; but I believe Jesus was speaking of something above these things. I believe His ultimate heart is as he asked us to pray, "*Manifest your kingdom on earth*:"

> **Luke 11:1** *One day, as Jesus was in prayer, one of his disciples came over to him as he finished and said, "Would you teach us a model prayer that we can pray, just like John did for his disciples?"* **2** *So Jesus taught them this prayer: "Our heavenly Father,*

> *may the glory of your name be the center on which*
> *our life turns. May your Holy Spirit come upon us*
> *and cleanse us. Manifest your kingdom on earth.* **3**
> *And give us our needed bread for the coming day.*
> **4** *Forgive our sins as we ourselves release forgiveness*
> *to those who have wronged us. And rescue us every*
> *time we face tribulations.*

This means more than just possessing abundance. It means one can see the resources of heaven released upon earth with miraculous power in such a way that it leaves a testimony of God's ability to overcome any circumstance.

Beautiful faces.

CHAPTER 3

To Know Him

Matthew 2:1 *Jesus was born in Bethlehem near Jerusalem during the reign of King Herod. After Jesus' birth a group of spiritual priests from the East came to Jerusalem* **2** *and inquired of the people, "Where is the child who is born king of the Jewish people? We observed his star rising in the sky and we've come to bow before him in worship."* **3** *King Herod was shaken to the core when he heard this, and not only him, but all of Jerusalem was disturbed when they heard this news.* **4** *So he called a meeting of the Jewish ruling priests and religious scholars, demanding that they tell him where the promised Messiah was prophesied to be born.* **5** *"He will be born in Bethlehem, in the land of Judah,"* they told him. "Because the prophecy states: **6** And you, little Bethlehem, are not insignificant among* *the clans of Judah, for out of you will emerge the Shepherd-King of my people Israel!"* **7** *Then Herod secretly summoned the spiritual priests from the East to ascertain the exact time the star first appeared.* **8** *And he told them, "Now go to Bethlehem and carefully look there for the child, and when you've found him, report to me so that I can go and bow down and worship him too."* **9** *And so they left, and on their way to Bethlehem, suddenly the same star they had seen in the East reappeared! Amazed, they watched as it went ahead of them and stopped directly over the place where the child was.* **10** *And when they saw the star, they were so ecstatic that they shouted and celebrated with unrestrained joy.* **11** *When they came into the house and saw the young child with Mary, his mother, they were overcome. Falling to the ground at his feet they worshiped him. Then they opened their treasure boxes full of gifts and presented him with gold, frank-incense, and myrrh.* **12** *Afterward they returned to their own country by another route because God had warned them in a dream not to go back to Herod.*

A few of things of note: (1) In verse 3 of this passage, it says that Herod, when hearing of the wise men making inquiry about the new king, was shaken to the core, and all of Jerusalem with him. Everyone in Jerusalem had heard what was going on with these visitors from the east. (2) When Herod called the chief priests and scribes, he asked them where the promised Messiah was to be born. Herod knew this was not just some next-in-line king, but the very Christ himself. The chief priests and scribes were well versed on the birth of the Christ and gave Herod the prophecy that He was to be born in Bethlehem. (3) Israel, as a nation, had been waiting for their messiah or Christ for hundreds of years, conservatively speaking; and the walking distance from Jerusalem to Bethlehem is approximately 8.5 km or just over 5 miles. I find it interesting that no one of all of the Jerusalemites, who were aware of this inquiry by the wise men to the point of being troubled, felt a need to go this distance (less than 2 hours' walk) to find out if what they were hearing from these wise men was true. It says in verse 8 that Herod sent the wise men to find the young child.

Why not? Why didn't anyone besides these wise men go? On pondering this question, the Lord began to speak to me that the mindset of those in Jerusalem at that time was that things had always been this way. "The Messiah did not come in my grandparents' day, or in my parents' day, so why should anything be different now?" We can get into a mode where we lose our expectation for God to move or we stop really believing for His promises. There can sometimes be nothing in us that responds to hearing the good news of something He's doing or has done.

But God's heart is that we're in constant expectation of His goodness. When we know Him, we'll expect to see His goodness; and God wants to be known. He wants friends that know Him. He can't do or be anything but good. It is His nature. The book of Jeremiah, chapter 9, says:

> **23** *This is what the Lord says: "Don't let the wise boast in their wisdom, or the powerful boast in their power, or the rich boast in their riches. **24** But those who wish to boast should boast in this alone: that they truly know me and understand that I am the Lord*

> *who demonstrates unfailing love and who brings*
> *justice and righteousness to the earth, and that I de-*
> *light in these things. I, the Lord, have spoken!* (NLT)

The Lord states in this passage that knowing Him is something to be grateful for. We can boast in knowing Him, that others may know that He is a God who can be and wants to be known. Jesus expressed His desire to be known when speaking to His disciples. He says this to Philip in the Gospel of John, chapter 14:

> **8** *Philip spoke up, "Lord, show us the Father, and*
> *that will be all that we need!"* **9** *Jesus replied, "Philip,*
> *I've been with you all this time and you still don't*
> *know who I am? How could you ask me to show*
> *you the Father, for anyone who has looked at me has*
> *seen the Father.* **10** *Don't you believe that the Father*
> *is living in me and that I am living in the Father?*
> *Even my words are not my own but come from my*
> *Father, for he lives in me and performs his miracles*
> *of power through me.*

Jesus issues the question, *"…you still don't know who I am?"* He is asking in relationship to the amount of close personal time He has spent with them. Part of His mission was that they would know Him and, as a result, know the Father, because He was in the Father and the Father in Him.

The book of Hebrews, chapter 11, verse 19, speaks of Abraham and the promise God had given him about his son Isaac, who was to be the one through whom Abraham would become the father of many nations. It says that when Abraham was asked of God to put this promise to death by sacrificing Isaac's young life on the altar,

> **19** *Abraham's faith made it logical to him that God could raise Isaac from the dead, and symbolically, that's exactly what happened.*

As I see it, Abraham's mindset was, "*I don't know how you're going to do this God, but I'm willing to die to this because I know you're a good God and can only do good things. You are going to honor your promise because you are not a man that you should lie, but you are faithful to your word and the good purpose you have over my life.*"

It had been 400 years without a prominent public prophetic voice to the nation of Israel in the time when Jesus was conceived of the Holy Spirit. There were those who experienced prophetically hearing from God, however, in a time of lack of the prophetic. Simeon experienced this during that time. The Bible just calls him a resident in Jerusalem and says:

> **Luke 2:25** *As they came to the temple to fulfill this requirement, an elderly man was there waiting— a resident of Jerusalem whose name was Simeon. He was a very good man, a lover of God who kept himself pure, and the Spirit of holiness rested upon him. Simeon believed in the imminent appearing of the one called "The Refreshing of Israel."* **26** *For the Holy Spirit had revealed to him that he would not see death before he saw the Messiah, the Anointed One of God.*

Not only did Simeon get the download that the Christ, whom the nation had been waiting to see for so long, was to be born in his lifetime; but when Jesus was brought by His parents into the temple at 8 days old (when most babies of the same nationality look pretty similar), Simeon, without announcement, with no heavenly host, no star, or any supernatural glorious manifestation, recognized the Christ in infant form. Anna, the prophetess did the same,

> **Luke 2:38** *While Simeon was prophesying over Mary and Joseph and the baby, Anna walked up to them and burst forth with a great chorus of praise to God for the child. And from that day forward she told everyone in Jerusalem who was waiting for their redemption that the anticipated Messiah had come!*

These are breakthrough individuals.

Another example of one who broke through is Mary, the mother of Jesus. When Jesus was 12 years old, the Gospel of Luke, chapter 2, says:

> **42** *When Jesus turned twelve, his parents took him to Jerusalem to observe the Passover, as was their custom.* **43** *A full day after they began their journey home, Joseph and Mary realized that Jesus was missing.* **44** *They had assumed he was somewhere in their entourage, but he was nowhere to be found. After a frantic search among relatives and friends,* **45** *Mary and Joseph returned to Jerusalem to search for him.* **46** *After being separated from him for three days, they finally found him in the temple, sitting among the Jewish teachers, listening to them and asking questions.* **47** *All who heard Jesus speak were astounded at his intelligent understanding of all that*

was being discussed and at his wise answers to their questions. **48** *His parents were shocked to find him there, and Mary scolded him, saying, "Son, your father and I have searched for you everywhere! We have been worried sick over not finding you. Why would you do this to us?"* **49** *Jesus said to them, "Why would you need to search for me? Didn't you know that it was necessary for me to be here in my Father's house, consumed with him?"* **50** *Mary and Joseph didn't fully understand what Jesus meant.* **51** *Jesus went with them back home to Nazareth and was obedient to them. His mother treasured Jesus' words deeply in her heart.*

In verse 49, Jesus questioned why they didn't know.

Verse 51 says that He went with them back home to Nazareth and was obedient to them, but his mother kept all these words deeply in her heart. The word "kept," in the original Greek here, is defined as to keep continually or carefully. I believe Mary could not get away from what Jesus said.

Fast forward 18 years. Jesus was at a wedding with His disciples, and His mother was there. The wine being served had run out. The Gospel of John, chapter 2, verse 3, tells us what Mary said to Jesus:

John 2:1 *Now on the third day there was a wedding feast in the Galilean village of Cana, and the mother of Jesus was there.* **2–3** *Jesus and his disciples were all invited to the banquet, but with so many guests in attendance, they ran out of wine. And when Mary realized it, she came to him and asked, "They have no wine, can't you do something about it?"* **4** *Jesus* replied, "My dear one, don't you understand that if I do this, it won't change anything for you, but it will change everything for me! My hour of unveiling my power has not yet come." **5** Mary then went to the servers and told them, "Whatever Jesus tells you, make sure that you do it!" **6** Now there were six stone water pots standing nearby. They were meant to be used for the Jewish washing rituals. Each one held about 20 gallons or more. **7** Jesus came to the servers and told them, "Fill the pots with water, right up to the very brim." **8** Then he said, "Now fill your pitchers and take them to the master of ceremonies." **9** And when they poured out their pitcher for the master of ceremonies to sample, the water became wine! When he tasted the water that became wine, the master of ceremonies was impressed. (Although he didn't know where the wine had come from, but the servers knew.) **10** He called the bridegroom over and said to him, "Every host serves his best wine first until everyone has had a cup or two, then he serves the wine of poor quality. But you, my friend, you've reserved the most exquisite wine until now!" **11** This miracle in Cana was the first of the many extraordinary miracles Jesus performed in Galilee. This was a sign revealing his glory, and his disciples believed in him.

Mary noticed there was a problem in the wedding. She was sensing something was going on that was bigger than this immediate problem. There was something that was about to happen. She was feeling a need to prepare for something God was about to do. What I like about Mary is that she didn't just keep this feeling to herself. She invited others to be a part of the breakthrough, saying to the servants, "*Whatever Jesus tells you, make sure that you do it!*" She saw breakthrough about to spring forth, and she saw a new thing that God was wanting to introduce. She said, "Get ready!" By this, Mary became a catalyst in initiating Jesus' miracle ministry. God used a regular human to bring one of the greatest breakthroughs the world has ever seen, even in the face of what sounded like opposition from Jesus himself. (verse 4: "*My hour of unveiling my power has not yet come.*") Breakthrough people know their God and His heart. I believe this was a test of Mary's heart. *Didn't you know that it was necessary for me to be here?* "Are you tracking with what's going on with me now Mary, are you with Me? Can we do this?"

Mary had a new understanding of who Jesus was.

God also spoke to the woman with the issue of blood:

> **Matthew 9:20** *Suddenly, a woman came from behind Jesus and touched the tassel of his prayer shawl for healing. She had been suffering from continual bleeding for twelve years, but had faith that Jesus could heal her.*

He also spoke to the centurion about who Jesus was and to the Syrophoenician woman whose daughter was possessed with a demon.

I believe that according to the Gospel of John, chapter 5, verses 19-20, God is speaking to his people, wanting his people to be what I call a 'breakthrough people', a people who partner with Him to introduce revelation that we've not yet seen of God into their generation, and to bring breakthrough for the generations to come.

> **John 5:19** *So Jesus said, "I speak to you timeless truth. The Son is not able to do anything from himself or through my own initiative. I only do the works that I see the Father doing, for the Son does the same works as his Father.* **20** *"Because the Father loves his Son so much, he always reveals to me everything that he is about to do. And you will all be amazed when he shows me even greater works than what you've seen so far!*

God wants us to see the things that aren't seen and partner with Him to see those things come into existence. In other words, if you have faith as a grain of mustard seed, you can see something that already exists move; but if your faith is great, you can see things that don't even exist move from the heavens into the place of existence where you are. You can become a partner in creating with God, seeing His will done on earth as it is in Heaven. Jesus said he did only those things He saw the Father do, which means that he saw the will of the Father about things that didn't even exist and partnered with the Father to see those things come into being.

In the Gospel of John, chapters 8 and 15, Jesus talks about having revelation about what the Father was doing:

> **John 8:38** *Yet the truths I speak I've seen and received in my Father's presence. But you are doing what you've learned from your father!"*

> **John 15:15** *I have never called you 'servants,' because a master doesn't confide in his servants, and servants don't always understand what the master is doing. But I call you my most intimate friends, for I reveal*

to you everything that I've heard from my Father.

Walking with God in this way is ministry born out of relationship. It isn't just doing, though that can be done, as it says in the Epistle to the Romans, chapter 11, verse 29, *"And when God chooses someone and graciously imparts gifts to him, they are never rescinded."* One can function in what God has blessed them with, even if not walking with Him at that moment. People who don't know Him do this all the time. However, God's ultimate goal in ministry is partnering. He's after being with us. He's in love with us. In the Gospel of John, chapter 15, verse 15, Jesus says, *"servants don't always understand what the master is doing. But I call you my most intimate friends, for I reveal to you everything that I've heard from my Father."* God wants friends. He wants a bride who is His best friend, a bride with whom He can share His intimate secrets as well as the new things He's about to do.

Because Jesus walked in the ultimate form of God's desire for relationship with man, Jesus saw people being healed before they were. He had been in communication with the Father about it. In the Gospel of John, chapter 9, there is another example of Jesus bringing breakthrough:

> **32** *Yet who has ever heard of a man born blind that was healed and given back his eyesight?* **33** *I tell you, if this man isn't from God, he wouldn't be able to heal me like he has!"*

The fact that the world had never seen a remedy for a man born blind was not a problem for Jesus. *What is the Father saying? What is the Father doing in this circumstance, here and now?* That is how we need to see our own challenges. We often look at our challenges from the standpoint of what has been. Jesus looked at this and other issues from the standpoint of what the Father was saying, and not just what had been, but what *would be* according to what He heard from the Father.

The Book of Isaiah, chapter 9, verse 7 speaks of His kingdom being constantly established. It does not pause; it does not retreat; there are no breaks; it's constantly taking new ground. It didn't stop in your mother's generation, in your grandmother's generation, or ever before that.

> **Isaiah 9:7** *Great and vast is his dominion. He will bring immeasurable peace and prosperity. He will rule on David's throne and over David's kingdom to establish and uphold it by promoting justice and righteousness from this time forward and forevermore. The marvelous passion that the Lord Yahweh, Commander of Angel Armies, has for his people will ensure that it is finished!*

New ground. That's what dreams are for. Your dreams matter to God and many times come from Him, and they are the very thing He's called you to introduce to your generation. Many times these are the intimate secrets God is revealing to His friends. Not that God doesn't cause people who don't know Him to dream big dreams, but it is so much more relationally fulfilling when the things you want to do can be done with a great friend – someone who is equally as excited about what you want as you are. You like the same things because you are alike in so many ways. Jonah knew God was going to forgive the people of Nineveh. Moses knew God didn't want to wipe out the children of Israel. Abraham knew God's heart was to spare Sodom and Gomorrah, and He stood before God on their behalf. They knew His heart, and I believe He loved that. It also demonstrates areas where

He's made us like Jesus.

What are you believing for that has never happened? Go after the King. An approximate 5-mile journey is all there was from Jerusalem to Bethlehem. The wise men were the only ones who made the journey. For us, we may have to seek the King also, to be a part of Him revealing Himself in ways we haven't seen.

> **Ezekiel 36:37** *"This is what the Sovereign Lord says: I am ready to hear Israel's prayers and to increase their numbers like a flock.*
>
> **Psalm 2:8** *Ask me to give you the nations and I will do it, and they shall become your legacy. Your domain will stretch to the ends of the earth.*

Partner with Him.

Special hugs from Shadrach.

CHAPTER 4

God's Heart for Intimate Connection

I'll say it again because it's so true. God is so in love with us. Let's look at what being in love looks like. Why did God put John the Baptist, the "voice of one crying in the wilderness" in a place outside of where the people usually were? Logically, if you are sending someone who is to broadcast the greatest news there has ever been, you would put him in a more common place. If it were us, John would have been the voice of one crying in the marketplace or in the theater—some place that people would actually see him. Along the same line of thought, the book of Mark, chapter 6, says that as Jesus was walking on the water toward His disciples who were struggling to row through the storm they were in, He made as though He would walk by them. It is interesting that Jesus, who put them into the boat and saw them toiling and rowing, decided not to go directly to them but make as though He was going to pass them by. This is because the Lord doesn't always want to do everything for us all the time.

For example, when I proposed to my beautiful bride, Robin,

I purchased a nice ring, planned a date, bought dinner for us, and took her to a scenic spot that I thought would be memorable. Then the moment came, and I got down on one knee, and asked the big question. Now, if there was no response from her, if she was looking around at the scenery, she was texting on her phone, she was focused on how good the food was, etc., I would have been somewhat disappointed. Say, she responded with a passive, "Sure, I guess so. Why not?" Then, I would have had to pick up her hand, pull her ring finger forward and place the ring on her limp hand that she had put no effort into placing before me. Well, that would have lacked a bit of fulfillment for me.

In the same way, the Lord looks for a response when he reveals Himself to us. In other words, whenever there is a revelation of the Lord, He is extending an invitation to come where He is. So Peter responded in the correct fashion by saying "Lord, if it is you, ask me to come out on the water." I believe Peter's response here is bridal, in a sense. *Lord, I want to be where you are. The things that are meaningful to you are meaningful to me.* These are elements of a truly romantic moment. Jesus says, "Come." I believe this brought a great measure of pleasure to the heart of the Lord. This was a moment of romance. The Epistle to the Ephesians, chapter 5, verse 32, says that a marriage is a picture of Jesus and His church. Jesus is the most romantic Husband there is. And so, in this moment, He was inviting those He loved into this experience with Him. This was a special moment, one never seen before. The Lord had wanted them to experience something new that He was doing. He wanted them to experience it with Him. It is the same with us; when there is something new we're doing, we want to experience it with those we love.

The Lord likes to reveal Himself in breakthrough ways. And He likes to do it with His friends. Can He show you what

He wants to do that hasn't been seen or experienced? Can you see Him breaking through in areas of our world that have not experienced Him? If you have a passion to see breakthrough, the Lord may be inviting you to be the vessel through whom he brings it into existence for His glory.

Let's go back to His heart for us to experience Him and all that He is—in other words, the fulfillment of the phrase from the Gospel of Matthew, chapter 6, verse 10, *"on earth, just as it is fulfilled in heaven."*—and then look at this passage in the Gospel of Mark, chapter 11:

> **11** *Jesus rode through the gates of Jerusalem and up to the temple. After looking around at everything, he left for Bethany with the Twelve to spend the night, for it was already late in the day.* **12** *The next day, as he left Bethany, Jesus was feeling hungry.* **13** *He noticed a leafy fig tree in the distance, so he walked over to see if there was any fruit on it, but there was none—only leaves (for it wasn't yet the season for bearing figs).* **14** *Jesus spoke to the fig tree, saying, "No one will ever eat fruit from you again!" And the disciples overheard him.* **15** *When they came into Jerusalem, Jesus went directly into the temple area and overturned all the tables and benches of the merchants who were doing business there. One by one he drove them all out of the temple courts, and they scattered away, including the money changers and those selling doves.* **16** *And he would not allow them to use the temple courts as a thoroughfare for carrying their merchandise and their furniture.* **17** *Then he began to teach the people, saying, "Does*

not the Scripture say, 'My house will be a house of prayer for all the world to share'? But you have made it a thieves' hangout!" **18** *When the chief priests and religious scholars heard this, they began to hatch a plot as to how they could eliminate Jesus. But they feared him and his influence, because the entire crowd was carried away with astonishment by his teaching.* **19** *So he and his disciples spent the nights outside the city.* **20** *In the morning, they passed by the fig tree that Jesus spoke to and it was completely withered from the roots up.* **21** *Peter remembered and said to him, "Teacher, look! That's the fig tree you cursed. It's now all shriveled up and dead."* **22** *Jesus replied, "Let the faith of God be in you!* **23** *Listen to the truth I speak to you: If someone says to this mountain with great faith and having no doubt, 'Mountain, be lifted up and thrown into the midst of the sea,' and believes that what he says will happen, it will be done.* **24** *This is the reason I urge you to boldly believe for whatever you ask for in prayer—believe that you have received it and it will be yours.*

Verse 13 says it wasn't yet the season for bearing figs. It seems kind of cruel to the tree to curse it if it wasn't even fig season. Should it be expected to produce fruit, given that God made the seasons and the elements weren't conducive to bearing fruit during this time?

I believe this passage in the Gospel of Mark, chapter 11, has to do with the prayer that Jesus taught us to pray in the Gospel of Matthew, chapter 6, verse 10, asking, *"Manifest your kingdom realm, and cause your every purpose to be fulfilled on earth, just as it is fulfilled in heaven.",* and that it implies Jesus wants that parallel.

In the book of Revelation, chapter 22, it says:

> **1** *Then the angel showed me the river of the water of life, flowing with water clear as crystal, continuously pouring out from the throne of God and of the Lamb.* **2** *The river was flowing in the middle of the street of the city, and on either side of the river was the Tree of Life, with its twelve kinds of ripe fruit according to each month of the year. The leaves of the Tree of Life are for the healing of the nations.*

In this heavenly atmosphere, as John was taken up in the Spirit, the tree that he notes seeing is one that bears multiple kinds of fruit all year long, independent of seasons. This is what I believe Jesus was longing for: "On earth as it is in heaven." Ultimately, I believe this is a picture for us as His people, whom He says will bear much fruit. He's not looking for us to be a fruit-bearing source that is dependent on outward conditions to bear. The heavenly tree bears fruit because its source is supernatural. This is what I believe is God's desire for us, that in every situation, in all conditions, we are those that are constantly bearing fruit: the fruit of His Spirit, the fruit of souls. The Bible talks about praise being the fruit of our lips. There is constant fruit, or life, being produced that others can experience because we are accessing the source of Heaven, Jesus himself, who did not rely on anything earthly to produce what was Heavenly. His source was God the Father. Jesus is the pattern example of fruitfulness. In any and all circumstances, in season and out of season, the Life of the Father is shown through Him.

When we were deciding on a name for the home the Lord

led us to open for our sons in the Congo who had found themselves estranged from their loved ones for various reasons, the Lord began speaking of a fruitfulness picture to me. It was in my heart in a strong way right before I was to facilitate a meeting with our team members. As we began the meeting with prayer, one of our team members, Michele, began sharing how the Lord was showing her a vision of a river coming from the throne of God, which was the irrigation system for the supernatural tree. Another team member began telling us of how the name that was in her heart was the name for a tree that in Congo was known for its all-weather fortitude. The Baobab tree, known as the Tree of Life, is not affected by the seasons but is constantly producing throughout the year. I then shared what the Lord had put in my heart out of this passage, and we knew what the Lord's heart was: not that we would have a great name for a house, but that the Lord was raising up our sons to be those who are givers of Life, not affected by the conditions they come from or by those they would come against, but constantly bearing fruit because they are drawing from a different source—Jesus.

The Apostle Paul is another example, in that he was able to say in the Epistle to the Philippians, chapter 4:

> **12** *I know what it means to lack, and I know what it means to experience overwhelming abundance. For I'm trained in the secret of overcoming all things, whether in fullness or in hunger.* **13** *And I find that the strength of Christ's explosive power infuses me to conquer every difficulty.*

Paul knew the source of navigating through life successfully: *"Christ's explosive power infuses me"*.

CHAPTER 5
Believing What God Said and Says

Obviously one of the ways we can miss or minimize what the Lord has for us is by listening to the enemy. Here is an example in the scripture of how that process can play out. In the Gospel of Matthew, chapter 4, it says:

> **1** *Afterward, the Holy Spirit led Jesus into the lonely wilderness in order to reveal his strength against the accuser by going through the ordeal of testing.* **2** *And after fasting for forty days, Jesus was extremely weak and famished.* **3** *Then the tempter came to entice him to provide food by doing a miracle. So he said to Jesus, "How can you possibly be the Son of God and go hungry? Just order these stones to be turned into loaves of bread."* **4** *He answered, "The Scriptures say: Bread alone will not satisfy, but true life is found in every word, which constantly goes forth from God's mouth."*

What the enemy said here, in short, was "*Since you are the Son of God, you shouldn't have to be out here in the middle of nowhere starving like this. Let's see if you are the Son of God. You deserve better than this. Go ahead and capitalize on your privilege; gratify the areas of dissatisfaction you're experiencing; don't stay in survival mode; this is not who you are.*" Of course, the temptation is to do this outside of connection with the Father. Jesus responded by quoting what is written, that bread alone will not satisfy, but true life is found in every word which constantly goes forth from God's mouth.

In some Bible translations, the Gospel of Matthew, chapter 4, verse 4, has the familiar phrase, "Man shall not live by bread alone…" The word "live" in Jesus' response has a future tense to it. Jesus is saying that He is not just after what He might get in the moment; He is saying that man shall not "live", meaning live in the way he was designed to live or experience the purpose for which he was created, which is not by satisfying the here and now only but by feasting on what God is saying. He is saying He is after the whole package, not just the now; He was after the purpose for which He came. That moment of need was not to define Him. Even though He had need and was not in a state of comfort, His purpose was higher; and He preferred God's will over his comfort. He would experience all of the purpose for which He came, and for that He would endure. Jesus preferred to do things in the way His Father wanted them done because the result would be so much greater.

Jesus fed on what His Father was saying in that moment. We would do well following and believing as well.

> **Romans 10:17** *Faith, then, is birthed in a heart that responds to God's anointed utterance of the Anointed One.*

One of the challenges of faith is defeating fear. I like how David says in the Psalms, "I will not be afraid." He purposed within what He would do related to situations that would seem naturally fearful. I love this. I believe Judas Iscariot, one of Jesus' disciples, fell prey to fear and insecurity. It says of Judas in the Gospel of John, chapter 12:

> **1** *Six days before the Passover began, Jesus went back to Bethany, the town where he raised Lazarus from the dead.* **2** *They had prepared a supper for Jesus. Martha served, and Lazarus and Mary were among those at the table.* **3** *Mary picked up an alabaster jar filled with nearly a liter of extremely rare and costly perfume—the purest extract of nard and she anointed Jesus' feet. Then she wiped them dry with her long hair. And the fragrance of the costly oil filled the house.* **4** *But Judas the locksmith, Simon's son, the betrayer, spoke up and said,* **5** *"What a waste! We could have sold this perfume for a fortune and given the money to the poor!"* **6** *(In fact, Judas had no heart for the poor. He only said this because he was a thief and in charge of the money case. He would steal money whenever he wanted from the funds given to support Jesus' ministry.)*

Judas took from the money case. How is it that one who was in the presence of absolute love, absolute care, one who watched provision, healing, comfort, and restoration take place on a regular basis, could be so blind? Judas was a participant in some of these things taking place in the lives of others; how could he feel as though he was not cared for in the area of finance to the degree that he had to fend for himself? For some reason,

Judas thought that what Jesus had for him just wasn't enough, so he had to make sure he was taken care of. How could there be better care for him than the love that was so available to him all day every day?

This same mindset Judas had can cause us to find our security in things and money rather than in Jesus. Jesus knew that Judas would struggle with this responsibility but still made him the treasurer of the group, giving him a chance to choose to trust Him.

God has natural provision for us; but when our trust and security is in Him, it comes in ways that are so much more fulfilling. This is why we can never say, "I cannot go after my dreams because of money or provision." Where is our trust? If God said to do something, He knows how much we have and whether it's enough or not. He has factored into the equation His supernatural ability to do anything at any time; and He will make sure that all our needs will be met according to His riches of glory, which are inexhaustible. There is no place of security that can be more peaceful than in the presence of Jesus, and yet Judas was deceived into believing that money had a greater measure of security.

CHAPTER 6
Aligning with His Heart

Matthew 9:27 *As Jesus left the house, two blind men began following him, shouting out over and over, "Son of David, show us mercy and heal us!"* **28** *And they followed him right into the house where Jesus was staying. So Jesus asked them, "Do you believe that I have the power to restore sight to your eyes?" They replied, "Yes Lord, we believe!"* **29** *Then Jesus put his hands over their eyes and said, "You will have what your faith expects!"* **30** *And instantly their eyes opened—they could see! Then Jesus warned them sternly, "Make sure that you tell no one what just happened!"* **31** *But unable to contain themselves, they went out and spread the news everywhere!*

When we were embarking on a project to open the house that we have in Kinshasa, Congo, the home of our sixteen sons who were once orphaned, the Lord spoke this Matthew 9 passage to us. We were basing the work we would be doing on the model of what our great friend Lilly Oyare established in the slums of Kibera, Kenya. The work she has done is phenomenal, and we wanted to see this work reproduced in different nations with similar conditions.

In the passage above, when the blind men came into the house, they came to him; and Jesus said to them, *"Do you believe that I have the power to restore sight to your eyes?"* I thought, and asked, "Lord, what difference did it make if they believed beforehand or not? They just wanted their sight." The Lord spoke to me that these men cried out to Him because of what they had heard He had done in other places. It's one thing to believe that Jesus can do something for someone, somewhere else, sometime; but it's a whole other thing to believe that He will do something for you right here, right now. He wanted them to get the full revelation of who He was: He was not just the God of those other times and places, but He is the God of the here and the now, no matter where we are.

I believe He wanted to cause us to always believe for the miraculous at all times. The Lord wanted us to believe that what He had done in the slums of Kibera, Kenya, He could also do in the areas of the same conditions in Kinshasa, Congo.

Sure enough, within a year of our first visit to Congo, we cut the ribbon on the home for our new sons. That is why I believe we can dream with great expectation.

God cares about our dreams. In fact, His word says in the Epistle to the Ephesians, chapter 3:

> **20** *Never doubt God's mighty power to work in you and accomplish all this. He will achieve infinitely*

*more than your greatest request, your most unbeliev-
able dream, and exceed your wildest imagination!
He will outdo them all, for his miraculous power
constantly energizes you.* **21** *Now we offer up to God
all the glorious praise that rises from every church in
every generation through Jesus Christ—and all that
will yet be manifest through time and eternity. Amen!*

He cares about the things we think about and is willing to
meet us in those things and go beyond the reach of our thoughts.
The above passage uses the word imagination. Imaginations or
dreams. I think of how Mary, the mother of Jesus, like most young
ladies, probably had a certain picture in mind of her wedding.
She probably had it all planned out. The type of garment she
would be adorned in. The setting. Wow, the place would be so
perfect. All of the family and friends would be there to celebrate
this long-anticipated moment when she would be joined to the
love of her life. However, during her betrothal to her loved one,
she had an uninvited, unexpected visitor by the name of Gabriel.
No call ahead, not even a knock on the door. He just showed
up with a greeting:

> **Luke 1:26-27** *During the sixth month of Elizabeth's
> pregnancy, the angel Gabriel was sent from God's
> presence to an unmarried girl named Mary, living
> in Nazareth, a village in Galilee. She was engaged
> to a man named Joseph, a true descendant of King
> David.* **28** *Gabriel appeared to her and said, "Grace
> to you, young woman, for the Lord is with you and
> so you are anointed with great favor."* **29** *Mary was
> deeply troubled over the words of the angel and be-
> wildered over what this may mean for her.* **30** *But*

the angel reassured her, saying, "Do not yield to your fear, Mary, for the Lord has found delight in you and has chosen to surprise you with a wonderful gift. 31 You will become pregnant with a baby boy, and you are to name him Jesus. 32 He will be supreme and will be known as the Son of the Highest. And the Lord God will enthrone him as King on his ancestor David's throne. 33 He will reign as King of Israel forever, and his reign will have no limit." 34 Mary said, "But how could this happen? I am still a virgin!" 35 Gabriel answered, "The Spirit of Holiness will fall upon you and almighty God will spread his shadow of power over you in a cloud of glory This is why the child born to you will be holy, and he will be called the Son of God. 36 What's more, your aged aunt, Elizabeth, has also become pregnant with a son. The 'barren one' is now in her sixth month. 37 Not one promise from God is empty of power, for nothing is impossible with God!"

"OK. Thank you, Lord. Maybe this will happen after I'm married and we can celebrate this together, Joseph and I." "Uh, no Mary, this is happening right now. Right in the middle of all your plans." *"Well, thank you, Lord. I know that, because this is your Son, the birth is going to be royal; it will be all I ever dreamed for the birth of my first child. Oh, how amazing it will be!"* "No, Mary. Your firstborn is going to come when you don't have a decent roof over your head; far from parents, aunts, uncles, and friends; not even in the sterile place into which all new moms expect to bring their beautiful new baby. Surprise, Mary, there is a nice stable planned for you!"

This would not be the end of the plan changes Mary would endure. However, I am convinced that in hindsight, and in light of eternity, Mary recognized the privilege she was given. She was able to walk in face-to-face relationship with the Living God in flesh as he nursed, grew, and developed as a human. His presence was in her home 24 hours a day, 7 days a week, in an incredible way. God, the Word, made flesh and dwelling among us (as Jesus is described in the Gospel of John, chapter 1, verse 14) was in her home for most of His time here on earth. I would be very surprised if Mary would say, after all she had experienced, that she would have changed a single thing. God has our highest and best in store, always.

THE SIGN OF JONAH

We can get discouraged sometimes thinking that we've blown it or that we're too far gone, too old, too this, or not enough of that. The story of Jonah is one of my favorite stories of how intent God is on fulfilling what He has purposed for us. God is committed. One day there were scribes talking to Jesus who began to seek a sign from Him.

> **Matthew 12:38** *Then a few Jewish scholars and Pharisees spoke up and said, "Teacher, why don't you perform a miraculous sign for us."* **39** *Jesus replied, "Only evil people who are unfaithful to God would demand a sign. There will be no sign given to you except the sign of the prophet Jonah.* **40** *For just like Jonah was in the belly of the huge sea creature for three days and three nights, so the Son of Man will be in the heart of the earth for three days and three nights.*

Jesus referred to Jonah as one who became an example of a revelation of what the Father's plan was for Jesus' earthly walk. How could Jonah do that? It was the grace of God that this happened because, as much as he could be, Jonah was in absolute rebellion to God. God had taken that into account beforehand and was still able to cause Jonah to be a revelation of the Lord Jesus Christ. God takes our failures into account. He is not surprised by or uninformed as to our failures, but somehow has planned victory for us despite how we may miss the mark and even when, like Jonah, we are in rebellion. This is why we should never be discouraged, because He's got it all mixed into His formula for our success.

Hallelujah!

WE ARE NOT ALONE

Sometimes we can feel as though we're alone in the fight, but we are not. Speaking to His disciples about the Holy Spirit, Jesus pictures this by saying in the Gospel of John, chapter 14:

> **25** *I am telling you this while I am still with you.*
> **26** *But when the Father sends the Spirit of Holiness, the One like me who sets you free, he will teach you all things in my name. And he will inspire you to remember every word that I've told you.*

I particularly like that Jesus says He (Holy Spirit) *"...will inspire you to remember every word that I've told you."* Holy Spirit is God. If there was anyone who could have arrived on the scene with an approach of, "Okay boys, I'm taking things from here. Just follow me and everything will be the way it should," that would be Him. But He relied upon what Jesus had already done in order to accomplish His mission. God does not discount what has gone before.

We think we're alone, not understanding sometimes that God has incorporated all the prayers, efforts, plowing, believing, reaching, and standing that the previous generations encountered and fought for. But we are not alone. We are standing on all that the saints before us have done, and we are blessed also with the momentum that comes from their efforts. These victories back us up as we press on to the fulfillment of the purpose God has for us. Because ultimately, this is God's plan that He has for all mankind; and we get to just be a part of it. It's all planned out, and He's given us a part to play; but by no means is it dependent on our personal know-how, grit, or self-help efforts to accomplish it. God has given us all the resources of heaven and earth to obtain the prize that Jesus paid for. Let's see it fulfilled.

Heloisa doing what she does so well.
Spreading the love of Jesus!

CHAPTER 7
Staying Connected

JOHN THE BAPTIST

God's ways are so different from the way we approach things. He has not designed us to be independent of Him. That is why we must remain connected. It's the ultimate fulfillment of life to love Him and love people, and the fulfillment of our specific purpose as well. When John the Baptist was to be born, the angel Gabriel visited his father Zechariah:

> **Luke 1:5** *During the reign of King Herod the Great over Judea, there was a Jewish priest named Zechariah who served in the temple as part of the priestly order of Abijah. His wife, Elizabeth, was also from a family of priests, being a direct descendant of Aaron.* **6** *They were both lovers of God, living virtuously and following the commandments of the Lord fully.* **7** *But they were childless since Elizabeth was barren,*

and now they both were quite old. **8–9** *One day, while Zechariah's priestly order was on duty and he was serving as priest, it happened by the casting of lots (according to the custom of the priesthood) that the honor fell upon Zechariah to enter into the Holy Place and burn incense before the Lord.* **10** *A large crowd of worshipers had gathered to pray outside the temple at the hour when incense was being offered.* **11** *All at once an angel of the Lord appeared to him, standing just to the right of the altar of incense.* **12** *Zechariah was startled and overwhelmed with fear.* **13** *But the angel reassured him, saying, "Don't be afraid, Zechariah! God is showing grace to you. For I have come to tell you that your prayer for a child has been answered. Your wife, Elizabeth, will bear you a son and you are to name him John.* **14** *His birth will bring you much joy and gladness. Many will rejoice because of him.* **15** *He will be one of the great ones in the sight of God. He will drink no wine or strong drink, but he will be filled with the Holy Spirit even while still in his mother's womb.* **16** *And he will persuade many in Israel to convert and turn back to the Lord their God.* **17** *He will go before the Lord as a forerunner, with the same power and anointing as Elijah the prophet. He will be instrumental in turning the hearts of the fathers in tenderness back to their children and the hearts of the disobedient back to the wisdom of their righteous fathers. And he will prepare a united people who are ready for the Lord's appearing."* **18** *Zechariah asked the angel, "How do you expect me* *to believe this? I'm an old man and my wife is too old to give me a child. What sign can you give me to prove this will happen?"* **19** *Then the angel said, "I am Gabriel. I stand beside God himself. He has sent me to announce to you this good news.* **20** *But now, since you did not believe my words, you will be stricken silent and unable to speak until the day my words have been fulfilled at their appointed time and a child is born to you. That will be your sign!"* **21** *Meanwhile, the crowds outside kept expecting him to come out. They were amazed over Zechariah's delay, wondering what could have happened inside the sanctuary.* **22** *When he finally did come out, he tried to talk, but he couldn't speak a word, and they realized from his gestures that he had seen a vision while in the Holy Place.* **23** *He remained mute as he finished his days of priestly ministry in the temple and then went back to his own home.* **24** *Soon afterward his wife, Elizabeth, became pregnant and went into seclusion for the next five months.* **25** *She said with joy, "See how kind it is of God to gaze upon me and take away the disgrace of my barrenness!"* **26–27** *During the sixth month of Elizabeth's pregnancy, the angel Gabriel was sent from God's presence to an unmarried girl named Mary, living in Nazareth, a village in Galilee. She was engaged to a man named Joseph, a true descendant of King David.* **28** *Gabriel appeared to her and said, "Grace to you, young woman, for the Lord is with you and so you are anointed with great favor."* **29** *Mary was deeply troubled over the words of the angel and* bewildered over what this may mean for her. **30** But the angel reassured her, saying, "Do not yield to your fear, Mary, for the Lord has found delight in you and has chosen to surprise you with a wonderful gift. **31** You will become pregnant with a baby boy, and you are to name him Jesus. **32** He will be supreme and will be known as the Son of the Highest. And the Lord God will enthrone him as King on his ancestor David's throne. **33** He will reign as King of Israel forever, and his reign will have no limit." **34** Mary said, "But how could this happen? I am still a virgin!" **35** Gabriel answered, "The Spirit of Holiness will fall upon you and almighty God will spread his shadow of power over you in a cloud of glory! This is why the child born to you will be holy, and he will be called the Son of God. **36** What's more, your aged aunt, Elizabeth, has also become pregnant with a son. The 'barren one' is now in her sixth month. **37** Not one promise from God is empty of power, for nothing is impossible with God!" **38** Then Mary responded, saying, "This is amazing! I will be a mother for the Lord! As his servant, I accept whatever he has for me. May everything you have told me come to pass." And the angel left her. **39** Afterward, Mary arose and hurried off to the hill country of Judea, to the village where Zechariah and Elizabeth lived. **40** Arriving at their home, Mary entered the house and greeted Elizabeth. **41** At the moment she heard Mary's voice, the baby within Elizabeth's womb jumped and kicked. And suddenly, Elizabeth was filled to overflowing with the Holy

Spirit! **42** *With a loud voice she prophesied with power: "Mary! You are a woman given the highest favor and privilege above all others. For your child is destined to bring God great delight.* **43** *How did I deserve such a remarkable honor to have the mother of my Lord come and visit me?* **44** *The moment you came in the door and greeted me, my baby danced inside me with ecstatic joy!* **45** *Great favor is upon you, for you have believed every word spoken to you from the Lord."* **46** *And Mary sang this song: "My soul is ecstatic, overflowing with praises to God!* **47** *My spirit bursts with joy over my life-giving God!* **48** *For he set his tender gaze upon me, his lowly servant girl. And from here on, everyone will know that I have been favored and blessed.* **49** *The Mighty One has worked a mighty miracle for me; holy is his name!* **50** *Mercy kisses all his godly lovers, from one generation to the next.* **51** *Mighty power flows from him to scatter all those who walk in pride.* **52** *Powerful princes he tears from their thrones and he lifts up the lowly to take their place.* **53** *Those who hunger for him will always be filled, but the smug and self-satisfied he will send away empty.* **54** *Because he can never forget to show mercy, he has helped his chosen servant, Israel,* **55** *Keeping his promises to Abraham and to his descendants forever."* **56** *Before going home, Mary stayed with Elizabeth for about three months.* **57** *When Elizabeth's pregnancy was full term, she gave birth to a son.* **58** *All her family, friends, and neighbors heard about it, and they too were overjoyed, for they realized that the Lord had* *showered such wonderful mercy upon her.* **59** *When the baby was eight days old, according to their custom, all the family and friends came together for the circumcision ceremony. Everyone was convinced that the parents would name the baby Zechariah, after his father.* **60** *But Elizabeth spoke up and said, "No, he has to be named John!"* **61** *"What?" they exclaimed. "No one in your family line has that name!"* **62** *So they gestured to the baby's father to ask what to name the child.* **63** *After motioning for a writing tablet, in amazement of all, he wrote, "His name is John."* **64** *Instantly Zechariah could speak again. And his first words were praises to the Lord.* **65** *The fear of God then fell on the people of their village, and the news of this astounding event traveled throughout the hill country of Judea. Everyone was in awe over it!*

The angel announced the name of the son to come as "John" in verse 13. It wasn't a suggestion or a foreknown announcement. It was a *"you are to…"* It was a command from Heaven. In verse 59, Elizabeth had friends and family around as it was the eighth day, the day for the child to be circumcised and to be named. Everyone who was there, with the exception of the child's parents, Elizabeth and Zechariah, suggested the boy be called after his father's name. Elizabeth immediately responded, *"No, he has to be named John!"* This was just as God commanded through the angel. The friends and cousins said, *"No one in your family line has that name!"* Then, they were so convinced that the boy shouldn't be named something other than a traditional name, a name that was from the family line, that they said they needed some input from his dad. So, in verse 62 they made signs to his father, asking how he would have the child named. Zechariah asked for a writing tablet and wrote on it, *"His name is John."*

Everyone was in awe. There was this command from Heaven, then the suggestion of the friends and family, then Elizabeth's refute, then a final declaration from Zechariah. Thinking about this, I felt the Lord causing me to question. "Wow, why is there all of this back and forth about the child's name? Lord, why did his name have to be John? Who cares what his name is? Why couldn't his name just be Zechariah, or Peter, Joshua or whatever?" Looking at the meaning of the name John in the Bible as it refers to John the Baptist, the name means: "Jehovah is a gracious giver." Why is that important?

When John the Baptist appeared on the scene and began to become public with a message, he began to get revelation that no one else had regarding who God was in the person of Jesus Christ. There were Simeon and Anna; however, being as old as they were when Jesus was born, they were surely gone by the time John's ministry began. At this point, God began to speak to John about Jesus, as it says in the Gospel of John, chapter 1:

> **15** *John taught the truth about him when he announced to the people, "He's the One! Set your hearts on him! I told you he would come after me, even though he ranks far above me, for he existed before I was even born."* **16** *And now out of his fullness we are fulfilled! And from him we receive grace heaped upon more grace!* **17** *Moses gave us the Law, but Jesus, the Anointed One, unveils truth wrapped in tender mercy.* **18** *No one has ever gazed upon the fullness of God's splendor except the uniquely beloved Son, who is cherished by the Father and held close to his heart.*

Now he has unfolded to us the full explanation of who God truly is **19** *There were some of the Jewish leaders who sent an entourage of priests and temple servants from Jerusalem to interrogate John. They asked him, "Who are you?"* **20** *John answered them directly, saying, "I am not the Messiah!"* **21** *"Then who are you?" they asked. "Are you Elijah?" "No," John replied. So they pressed him further, "Are you the prophet Moses said was coming, the one we're expecting?" "No," he replied.* **22** *"Then who are you?" they demanded. "We need an answer for those who sent us. Tell us something about yourself—anything!"* **23** *So, John answered them, "I am fulfilling Isaiah's prophecy: 'I am an urgent, thundering voice shouting in the desert—clear the way and prepare your hearts for the coming of the Lord Yahweh!'"* **24** *Then some members of the religious sect known as the Pharisees questioned John,* **25** *"Why do you baptize the people since you admit you're not the Christ, Elijah, or the Prophet?"* **26–27** *John answered them, "I baptize in this river, but the One who will take my place is to be more honored than I, but even when he stands among you, you will not recognize or embrace him! I am not worthy enough to stoop down in front of him and untie his sandals!"* **28** *This all took place at Bethany, where John was baptizing at the place of the crossing of the Jordan River.* **29** *The very next day John saw Jesus coming to him to be baptized, and John cried out, "Look! There he is—God's Lamb! He will take away the sins of the world!* **30** *I told you that a Mighty One* *would come who is far greater than I am, because he existed long before I was born!* **31** *My baptism was for the preparation of his appearing to Israel, even though I've yet to experience him."* **32** *Then, as John baptized Jesus he spoke these words: "I see the Spirit of God appear like a dove descending from the heavenly realm and landing upon him—and it rested upon him from that moment forward!* **33** *And even though I've yet to experience him, when I was commissioned to baptize with water God spoke these words to me, 'One day you will see the Spirit descend and remain upon a man. He will be the One I have sent to baptize with the Holy Spirit.'* **34** *And now I have seen with discernment. I can tell you for sure that this man is the Son of God."*

John had this conversation with Father God about Jesus, not seeming to have any knowledge of who Jesus was based on natural attributes of any kind. But he saw Jesus spiritually for who He really was, because of what the Father communicated to him. In verse 33, John said, *"And even though I've yet to experience him, when I was commissioned to baptize with water God spoke these words to me, 'One day you will see the Spirit descend and remain upon a man."* So, John records, in verse 34, *"And now I have seen with discernment. I can tell you for sure that this man is the Son of God."*

What does all of this mean? Well, in John's day, as I mentioned earlier, there was no national prophetic voice to Israel as a whole. In the past there had been prophets sent from God to the nation for the purpose of speaking and declaring God's call to His people to return to Him, or messages of some other nature. In this case, John is doing the same; however, his message is unique. John's message is, as the King James translation phrases it, "the Kingdom of Heaven is at hand." In other words, as I stated earlier, God is bringing His kingdom, the kingdom He wants to give to everyone, near.

But why the name John? Well, before John, the people of God kept the ceremonial law. They approached God based on their keeping of the law and sacrificing where there was a lack thereof. John began to get this revelation, not based on his credentials or his ability to adhere to the law, but by grace…just because *Jehovah is a gracious giver*. So, John was a message that things were changing. Things would be different with the once and for all true sacrifice for sins that Jesus would make for all mankind on the cross.

Now our approach to God is by faith in the permanent atonement that Jesus made. It was always God's desire that we approach Him based on His graciousness, never by our works. This is why we all fell short, because the law can never make anyone righteous. John presented God approaching man because He is gracious. This is how we can all come before Him. Jesus paid it all, graciously giving the result to us.

How does this relate to dreaming? Well, we as Christians know that we now approach God by grace. But if that is the case, and everything we receive from God comes by grace, then why do we not ask of God accordingly? If it's really not by our works, then there is no merit. There is, then, also no limit. If it's according to what Jesus has done, then there is no reason that we can't have all of what Jesus made available, all that He had. The heavens are the limit, which is another way of saying there is no limit. That was Jesus' mindset: "On earth as it is in Heaven." Jesus prayed for things this world had never seen. Those are the kinds of prayers we should pray. I believe that is why Jesus marveled at the request made by the centurion whose servant was sick.

THE CENTURION

The Gospel of Matthew, chapter 8, says:

> **5** *When Jesus entered the village of Capernaum, a captain in the Roman army approached him, asking for a miracle.* **6** *"Lord," he said, "I have a son who is lying in my home, paralyzed and suffering terribly."* **7** *Jesus responded, "I will go with you and heal him."* **8–9** *But the Roman officer interjected, "Lord, who am I to have you come into my house? I understand your authority, for I too am a man who walks under authority and have authority over soldiers who serve under me. I can tell one to go and he'll go, and another to come and he'll come. I order my servants and they'll do whatever I ask. So I know that all you need to do is to stand here and command healing over my son and he will be instantly healed."* **10** *Jesus was astonished when he heard this and said to those who were following him, "He has greater faith than anyone I've encountered in Israel!* **11** *Listen to what I am about to tell you. Multitudes of non-Jewish people will stream from the east and the west, to enter into the banqueting feast with Abraham, Isaac, and Jacob in the heavenly kingdom.* **12** *But many Israelites, born to be heirs of the kingdom, will be turned away and banished into the darkness where there will be bitter weeping and unbearable anguish."* **13** *Then Jesus turned to*

the Roman officer and said, "Go home. All that you have believed for will be done for you!" And his son was healed at that very moment.

It says in verse 10 that Jesus was astonished. This man asked Jesus for something that no one else was believing for. After the man left, Jesus then turned to the crowd that was following Him and made an example out of the centurion, saying, "*He has greater faith than anyone I've encountered...*" In other words, *I have not found someone who will believe me according the limitlessness of what I am able to do.*

All of us have seen people we call bodybuilders. They have a great physique, with massive muscles bulging out in places we never thought we would see muscles. They are incredibly strong. Now it would be ridiculous for me to ask a bodybuilder if he could pick up a five-pound barbell. Why? Because I can see how much he is able to lift, and that would certainly exceed five pounds. This centurion saw Jesus for who He really was and was able to ask accordingly, in such a way that it exceeded the faith Jesus had found elsewhere.

Now, there *is* no limit to what God is able to do, and I believe God is looking for someone to actually see who He really is, and then ask Him according to that. Who will be that one who asks in a way that others have not because they see in a way that others do not see? Who will then break through? Jesus made the centurion an example because this is what He is looking for, and I believe God wants to bring breakthrough into our world that we have never ever seen. Who will be the one to partner with God in prayer to bring it into being? Who will ask to see further? Will you?

CHAPTER 8

Jesus Is Committed to You

Even the bad can fulfill the good. The whole Bible is about Jesus. It's all about Him, the One who was and is and is to come. Two Old Testament prophecies from Daniel 9 and Zechariah 9 tell of Jesus' triumphant entry into Jerusalem not very long before his arrest and crucifixion. Without going into too much detail, Jesus' triumphant entry into Jerusalem, riding on a donkey, was foretold in such specificity that it was prophesied foretelling the very day that it would happen, and it did.

What I like about this prophecy is the way God made it come to pass. There were two sisters, Mary and Martha, who had a brother named Lazarus. The story in the Gospel of John, chapter 12, reads:

> **1** *Six days before the Passover began, Jesus went back to Bethany, the town where he raised Lazarus from the dead.* **2** *They had prepared a supper for Jesus. Martha served, and Lazarus and Mary were among*

> *those at the table. 3 Mary picked up an alabaster jar filled with nearly a liter of extremely rare and costly perfume—the purest extract of nard, and she anointed Jesus' feet. Then she wiped them dry with her long hair. And the fragrance of the costly oil filled the house. 4 But Judas the locksmith, Simon's son, the betrayer, spoke up and said, 5 "What a waste! We could have sold this perfume for a fortune and given the money to the poor!" 6 (In fact, Judas had no heart for the poor. He only said this because he was a thief and in charge of the money case. He would steal money whenever he wanted from the funds given to support Jesus' ministry.) 7 Jesus said to Judas, "Leave her alone! She has saved it for the time of my burial. 8 You'll always have the poor with you; but you won't always have me." 9 When the word got out that Jesus was not far from Jerusalem, a large crowd came out to see him, and they also wanted to see Lazarus, the man Jesus had raised from the dead.*

Verse 9 says that people came to this monumental event, not for Jesus' sake only, but also to see Lazarus, whom Jesus had raised from the dead. So, it is clear that God's heart for this event was that it would happen exactly how and when it did, because in the Gospel of Luke, chapter 19, it says:

> *37 As soon as he got to the bottom of the Mount of Olives, the crowds of his followers shouted with a loud outburst of ecstatic joy over all the mighty wonders of power they had witnessed. 38 They shouted over and over, "Highest praises to God for the one who*

comes as King in the name of the Lord! Heaven's peace and glory from the highest realm now comes to us!" **39** *Some Jewish religious leaders who stood off from the procession said to Jesus, "Teacher, you must order your followers at once to stop saying these things!"* **40** *Jesus responded, "Listen to me. If my followers were silenced, the very stones would break forth with praises!"*

Jesus said that if no one had participated, it still would have happened, even if non-human creation had to be engaged. The stones would cry out. God will fulfill His word. Having said that, I like the "how" of the fulfillment of this word: some came not only to see Jesus, but also to see Lazarus, whom Jesus had raised from the dead. So, Lazarus had a role to play in this great monumental event. What did Lazarus get to do? He got to get sick and die. Not that God caused Lazarus' sickness or death; but in His foreknowledge, He used that circumstance to fulfill His ultimate purpose in Jesus' entry into Jerusalem. Wow. We can never limit what God is able to do, even in what looks like the worst of times. God raised up Lazarus to be an influence in what the greater purpose of that day was. We don't even realize sometimes how the things that we experience feed into the greater purpose God has for mankind. What happened to Lazarus was so much bigger than him. It had to do with what God had for us also. What if your purpose is to have ramifications for future generations and will grow even bigger after your life has passed? That was the case for Abraham. His legacy is greater in today's generation than it was in his day. That was the case with most people in the scripture. They didn't know the significance their lives had. Just the same, I believe that we have no idea the level of impact God will bring through things He is initiating in our lives. I believe this is why it says in the Gospel of Matthew, chapter 25:

31 *"When the Son of Man appears in his majestic glory, with all his angels by his side, he will take his seat on his throne of splendor,* **32** *and all the nations will be gathered together before him. And like a shepherd who separates the sheep from the goats, he will separate all the people.* **33** *The 'sheep' he will put on his right side and the 'goats' on his left.* **34** *Then the King will turn to those on his right and say, 'You have a special place in my Father's heart. Come and experience the full inheritance of the kingdom realm that has been destined for you from before the foundation of the world!* **35** *For when you saw me hungry, you fed me. When you found me thirsty, you gave me something to drink. When I had no place to stay, you invited me in,* **36** *and when I was poorly clothed, you covered me. When I was sick, you tenderly cared for me, and when I was in prison you visited me.'* **37** *"Then the godly will answer him, 'Lord, when did we see you hungry or thirsty and give you food and something to drink?* **38** *When did we see you with no place to stay and invite you in? When did we see you poorly clothed and cover you?* **39** *When did we see you sick and tenderly care for you, or in prison and visit you?'* **40** *"And the King will answer them, 'Don't you know? When you cared for one of the least important of these my little ones, my true brothers and sisters, you* *demonstrated love for me.'*

There are things that the Lord pays attention to in our lives that have no significance to us, and yet the Lord feels they are worthy of acknowledging and even rewarding. We are in for a great awakening when it comes to how much the Father has prepared for those who love Him.

PRECIOUS

Each one of us is so special to the Father. I remember when our first child, our son, was born. We had all things planned as to how we were going to parent, and then the Lord began to speak to us about our children. He spoke to us out of the lives of Zechariah and Elizabeth. The way they named John was in opposition to what their peers and family felt their son should have been named. Because Zechariah and Elizabeth named their son, and parented beyond that, in partnership with what the Lord had to say over John's life, it gave John the momentum to step into what God had for him. Not that God couldn't have done what He wanted in John's life without Zechariah and Elizabeth, but God's intent is that we partner with Him in positioning things for what He has for the next generation. For that reason, the Lord spoke to us about the way we parent. It was not to be according to what society says is the best way to parent, although there is very good information out there on parenting. But in our case, God wanted us to partner with Him specifically according to what God had for our children. We knew we were to position things in their lives to allow them the ease of stepping into what He has for them. And now, for us that means creating an atmosphere in our home where our children can dream in a big way.

When we are childlike and belief isn't a second thought but, in today's terminology, "it is what it is," it is amazing how we begin to allow God to be God through us. I was on a trip to Congo without my family. They were at home going through their daily routines of school, domestic responsibilities, etc.; and they were praying for me at night before bedtime. During their time of prayer, God spoke to us. My daughter hears from the Lord in pictures or in other ways He chooses to communicate. So, one night while I was in Congo, the Lord showed my daughter a picture of an alligator and a turtle. She didn't wait on the Lord in some way that was like a monk in a monastery. She just simply paid attention, and in a few seconds that is what she saw. Well, she didn't know that I was just then in a restaurant in Congo, ordering what I had never eaten before in my life. A member of our team and I decided to be daring in branching out in new areas of cuisine. So, what did we order, but alligator and turtle? Through our daughter's prayer, the Lord encouraged us by showing us the level of detail in which He was involved in what we were doing. The Lord is causing both of my children to grow in their ability to hear and know Him. Dreams will be fulfilled in their lives.

At around age six my son began saying he wanted to be an inventor. When I first heard this, I thought, *"Aw, that's cute."* I thought, *"Go ahead, son; believe and pursue things most people think impossible."* The reason I had this initial response is that I didn't believe these kinds of things for myself—specific dreams.

But our son kept saying this over and over again, and then my wife had a dream. In the dream, my son was in a large store in our area, Target, and he was in line to buy tickets to the Superbowl. If you know anything about American sports, you know the Superbowl is considered the largest, most influential sporting event in our nation, and in the top five in all the world.

Later, the Lord spoke to us about this dream, that it meant our son was in line and on target for big things; and we as his parents weren't. This became part of a whole vision the Lord began to give us for children, and He invited us into it with Him. We are receiving and seeking Him for more of it for our children now: empowering them and other children with a world-changing mindset.

In this journey, the Lord first showed us that we can't impart a world—changing mindset to others if we don't believe that about ourselves. At first, we were saying our sons in the Congo would be raised up to be doctors, lawyers, or politicians; but our approach is now, "We are raising up world changers of all kinds to go into every area of the world." Yes, we *are* raising up doctors, lawyers, and politicians. But the Lord showed me that when I partner with him, I can change the world. I believe what he showed me about myself; therefore, I can impart this mindset to my sons.

Because we believe we have not yet seen all of who God is, we also believe that God wants to continue to demonstrate His greatness. So, there will be those who allow the Lord to use them to spearhead things that are innovative, inventive, creative, and things we have yet to conceive of—because God is still creating.

An analogy the Lord showed me is related to the smartphone, with all of its abilities. If one had been told a hundred years ago that it would become possible to hold a 3x5 inch device on one's hand and communicate face to face in real time with people in the farthest places of the world, it would have seemed impossible. But the smartphone did not create itself. There were people who believed for technology of this sort to become a reality and invested in its conception so that today we benefit from their pursuit of what they believed could happen. Again, our God says in the Epistle to the Ephesians, Chapter 3:

> **20** *Never doubt God's mighty power to work in you and accomplish all this. He will achieve infinitely more than your greatest request, your most unbelievable dream, and exceed your wildest imagination! He will outdo them all, for his miraculous power constantly energizes you.* **21** *Now we offer up to God all the glorious praise that rises from every church in every generation through Jesus Christ—and all that will yet be manifest through time and eternity. Amen!*

There is nothing God cannot do. I believe He's looking for friends with whom He can do some of those things that are above what we, as a whole, have believed for, so that we all can begin to believe Him for more. It's basically agreeing with who He really is.

CHAPTER 9
The Big Picture

DAVID, A BIG DREAMER

The Lord began to speak to my wife and me about becoming involved in anti-human trafficking. This came because of a trip we took to Redding, California, to a healing conference. I was sitting in my seat, which was an aisle seat, as a woman who was very inebriated in the Spirit was passing by. Her friend was trying to help her up the stairs as she was laughing and stumbling. When she reached my seat, she put her hand on my knee and began to tell me about how the Lord was sending my wife and me to nations, and how we would minister to pastors and leaders. She included in her pronouncement that we would empower women.

At this point, we had been involved in different aspects of missions, having visited a couple of nations; and it had been necessary to believe God in order to be able to get to those. Therefore, the woman's word seemed to be in line with what the

Lord had begun and in line with other similar words that He had spoken into our lives through people who didn't know us. The part that stood out this time was the empowering of women. It was unique enough that it caused me to ponder, since I had never considered that as something separate from anything else we had done. But because of the accuracy of the other details, I knew this was from God.

Not long after this, my aunt let me know she had a dream about my son. In the dream, she was in a big house; and she was looking for the ladies' room. As she was walking through the house looking, she saw my son, who was about six years old at the time. He told her, "I know where the ladies' room is." He then led her to a door and opened it. On the other side of the door was a harvest field; and in the field, there were white sheep. That was the dream; and when we asked the Lord to speak to us about it, He showed us it was connected to the empowering of women and that my aunt wasn't looking for the bathroom or the restroom, but the *ladies'* room. On the other side there were white sheep in a harvest field. So, He spoke to us that the ladies' room is this place behind closed doors where there are women who are sexually abused, but that this is a harvest field of those He wants to reap for Himself. And the way he sees them is not as those who have been defiled and dirty, as they are viewed by those who have treated them in this way; but God sees them as pure white sheep. White in the Bible speaks of purity. God sees them as those He will restore and cause to overcome all the effects of what their abusers have inflicted upon them. Pure. That's who these ladies are.

So, we began to do some research and found out that there are an estimated 27 million people trapped in slavery, or what we call human trafficking. I said in my heart, "Lord, 27 million people. How do you even begin to scratch the surface of something like that?" The Lord then began speaking to me out of the life of David in the Bible. In the book of 1 Samuel, chapter 17, as David and Goliath are facing off and declaring victory over each other, it reads:

> **41** *Goliath walked out toward David with his shield bearer ahead of him,* **42** *sneering in contempt at this ruddy-faced boy.* **43** *"Am I a dog," he roared at David, "that you come at me with a stick?" And he cursed David by the names of his gods.* **44** *"Come over here, and I'll give your flesh to the birds and wild animals!" Goliath yelled.* **45** *David replied to the Philistine, "You come to me with sword, spear, and javelin, but I come to you in the name of the Lord of Heaven's Armies—the God of the armies of Israel, whom you have defied.* **46** *Today the Lord will conquer you, and I will kill you and cut off your head. And then I will give the dead bodies of your men to the birds and wild animals, and the whole world will know that there is a God in Israel!* **47** *And everyone assembled here will know that the Lord rescues his people, but not with sword and spear. This is the Lord's battle, and he will give you to us!"* **48** *As Goliath moved closer to attack, David quickly ran out to meet him.* **49** *Reaching into his shepherd's bag and taking out a stone, he hurled it with his sling and hit the Philistine in the forehead. The stone sank in, and Goliath stumbled and fell face down on the ground.* **50** *So David triumphed over the Philistine with only a sling and a stone, for he*

had no sword. **51** *Then David ran over and pulled Goliath's sword from its sheath. David used it to kill him and cut off his head. When the Philistines saw that their champion was dead, they turned and ran.* **52** *Then the men of Israel and Judah gave a great shout of triumph and rushed after the Philistines, chasing them as far as Gath and the gates of Ekron. The bodies of the dead and wounded Philistines were strewn all along the road from Shaaraim, as far as Gath and Ekron.* (NLT)

In verse 46, David declares, "*Today the Lord will conquer you, and I will kill you and cut off your head. And then I will give the dead bodies of your men to the birds and wild animals, and the whole world will know that there is a God in Israel!*" One thing that struck me about this is that David says "I" *will give the dead bodies of your men…*, not "we". Listening to David's language, we understand that David was prepared to take on the entire Philistine army single handedly. How do we know this? Well, by looking at David's mighty men, whom he trained. In the book of Chronicles, they defeated whole armies single handedly. Where did they get the idea that they could do that, having come to David discontent, in debt, and distressed? They got the idea they could defeat whole armies from David.

One thing to recognize is that David did not take a head count and then decide he could take these Philistines. David had no idea how many of them there were, and it did not matter. In his mind, he could take them all. That is the mentality that the Lord spoke to us that we are to have in relationship to the numbers reported about trafficking. It doesn't matter how many need rescuing, God is big enough to turn this world upside down, if he wants, and then open the door for every single one. He is looking for people to be a part of the great victory that He is going to bring in delivering His lambs out of this trafficking industry.

The Lord graciously gave us another confirmation when my mother-in-law took my family on a trip to Yosemite Park here in California. On the last day, we were walking down a hill to the dining hall. As we walked, we were about 30 yards from our tent when my wife accidentally kicked a key out of the dirt on the ground. We looked down and picked it up. It happened that the number of the tent we were staying in was on this key. What's interesting is this kind of key wasn't being used anymore at this park because, obviously, if someone finds a key with a tent number on it, they have access to all of someone else's belongings. We were staying in an area where there were over six hundred tents condensed together. These tents were stationed with about six feet between those side by side, and about 25 feet before and behind. I thought it interesting that, after all the time that had passed since this kind of key was used, it would be found that close to our tent. It was not buried deep at all, and why were we the ones who happened to find it? It could have been any number, but it was the number of the tent we happened to be staying in. It all struck me as too ironic, and I couldn't get away from it.

The very next day, as we were sitting behind our good friend, Michele, in church, she turned around to us during the service and said, "You have to meet this friend of mine who's involved in helping the abused in Brazil." We love missions and enjoy talking about it with anyone, so we made an appointment and met with Michele's friend. A few days later, she took us to his office, just a few miles away. As we all sat down together to begin our interchange, Michele prayed; and without knowing what the Lord had been speaking to Robin and me about the trafficking issue within the context of David, she said, "Lord, how do we deal with this thing? It's such a David and Goliath issue." God was speaking to us again through this prayer. At the end of this meeting, this friend of Michele's invited us to accompany him and be a part of what He was doing in Brazil. We were very excited.

BACK TO THE KEY

I just couldn't get away from this thing. *Lord what is this key about?* The Lord led us to this passage in the book of Revelation, chapter 3:

> **7** *Write the following to the messenger of the congregation in Philadelphia, for these are the solemn words of the Holy One, the true one, who has David's key, who opens doors that none can shut and who closes doors that none can open:* **8** *I know all that you've done. Now I have set before you a wide-open door that none can shut...*

The Lord began to speak to us that He, the Lord Himself, as it says in verse 7, is He *"who has David's key, who opens doors that none can shut and who closes doors that none can open."* He then began to let us know that this opportunity that was extended to us to partner in what is taking place in Brazil was an invitation from Him, the one who holds the key of David. *He* has opened this door for us. It so happened that the one through whom he extended the invitation, the friend of Michele, was named David. This was the friend of our friend Michele. Needless to say, our hearts are now ablaze for what God has for the nation of Brazil, and in a big way. God himself has encouraged us, and we are dreaming in a big way; we are putting feet to the dream.

CHAPTER 10
Things in Heaven

Nicodemus

The Gospel of John says, in chapter 3:

> **1** *Now there was a prominent religious leader among the Jews named Nicodemus, who was part of the sect called the Pharisees and a member of the Jewish ruling council.* **2** *One night he discreetly came to Jesus and said, "Master, we know that you are a teacher from God, for no one performs the miracle signs that you do, unless God's power is with him."* **3** *Jesus answered, "Nicodemus, listen to this eternal truth: Before a person can perceive God's kingdom realm, they must first experience a rebirth."* **4** *Nicodemus said, "Rebirth? How can a gray-headed man be reborn? It's impossible for a man to go back into the womb a second time and be reborn!"* **5** *Jesus*

answered, "I speak an eternal truth: Unless you are born of water and Spirit-wind, you will never enter God's kingdom realm. 6 For the natural realm can only give birth to things that are natural, but the spiritual realm gives birth to supernatural life! 7 "You shouldn't be amazed by my statement, 'You must be born from above!' 8 For the Spirit-wind blows as it chooses. You can hear its sound, but you don't know where it came from or where it's going. So it is within the hearts of those who are Spirit-born!" 9 Then Nicodemus replied, "But I don't understand, what do you mean? How does this happen?" 10 Jesus answered, "Nicodemus, aren't you the respected teacher in Israel, and yet you don't understand this revelation? 11 I speak eternal truths about things I know, things I've seen and experienced—and still you don't accept what I reveal. 12 If you're unable to understand and believe what I've told you about the natural realm, what will you do when I begin to unveil the heavenly realm?

I love this passage because, in it, Nicodemus is pondering Jesus's identity and stepping out on what he believes about Him. Jesus begins to talk to Nicodemus about what He came to make available for Nicodemus. Jesus gives him a couple of examples that he is familiar with about nature: being born and wind blowing. Nicodemus expresses his struggle to grasp what Jesus is talking about.

He says in Verse 9, *"But I don't understand, what do you mean? How does this happen?"* Jesus' response in Verse 12 is, *"If you're unable to understand and believe what I've told you about the natural realm, what will you do when I begin to unveil the heavenly realm?"* In other words, "I am talking to you about things that can be compared to an earthly example, things you can see or feel. Nicodemus, if you are struggling to receive what I am speaking to you about these earthly things, what will you do if I begin to speak to you about things that have yet to come to be on earth (heavenly things that you don't yet have an example of)? …Will you be one who is a channel for the prototype of what God wants to do in certain areas? You see, Nicodemus, it is in my heart to talk to people about those things that can only be seen by the Spirit."

Jesus taught us in the Gospel of Matthew, chapter 6, verse 10, to pray "on earth as it is in Heaven" (NLT). Jesus' heart is to introduce into the earth things that have been in the Father's heart. I submit to you that the Holy Spirit wants to reveal those things to us and invite us to partner with God in seeing them come to be. Jesus knew that Lazarus' sickness was not going to leave him in a state of permanent death, and so he said to Lazarus' sisters, Mary and Martha, in the Gospel of John, chapter 11, verse 4, *"This sickness will not end in death for Lazarus, but will bring glory and praise to God. This will reveal the greatness of the Son of God by what takes place."* There was a revelation of Jesus as "the resurrection and the life" (as stated in the Gospel of John, chapter 11, verse 25, KJV) that the world had not seen and that the Father wanted to reveal. Jesus made this statement in the Gospel of John, chapter 11, verse 4, in partnership with the Father. The Spirit of God revealed to Jesus what the Father wanted to do even before it happened, and Jesus made Himself available to partner with this revelation. There are revelations of who God is that we have yet to see. God will call people to be a part of how He is revealed as the victorious one over every area of life.

If you're going to receive and enter into the kingdom of God, the place where God really rules, you're going to have to let go some of the things you think you understand and allow God to talk to you about things that you don't understand. These things are bigger than your understanding. They are where God becomes the ultimate source of your understanding. In the book of Proverbs, chapter 3, it says:

> **5** *Trust in the Lord completely, and do not rely on your own opinions. With all your heart rely on him to guide you, and he will lead you in every decision you make.*

This verse tells us there will be times when we will need the Lord's perspective on things, because our own will be completely insufficient. In other words, don't trust in anything you can come up with about this scenario; it is beyond what you have the ability to comprehend on your own.

The Pharisees would have done well to heed this verse, as they consistently tried to trap Jesus, thinking He would do or say one of two things; and yet Heaven's perspective was completely outside of their limited expectation. This was so often the case with Jesus' disciples as well, and we are no different. God's thoughts are higher than ours. Does that mean we can't think for ourselves? No. That is not God's intent. God gave us our minds; however, there are times when we as humans elevate our understanding in human terms. But by trusting God with all our hearts and seeking His understanding, and in all our ways acknowledging him, we ensure that He will be the one directing our paths.

In other words, there is a place that God wants to take us that we don't know how to get to except by listening to Him and trusting Him, because our own understanding won't get us there – to the kingdom where God rules. It reminds me of Adam and Eve in the garden, where they had to let go of their own understanding in order to live in all of what God had for them, but the devil came and told them that they could know something beyond God's knowledge.

Jesus did not want Nicodemus to marvel at the term "born again," but to understand its implications and consider it an earthly depiction of a heavenly – or spiritual – reality. Jesus was trying to explain greater works beyond any yet seen, works for which Nicodemus did not yet have a reference in his mind.

I was listening recently to a missionary speak about a miracle God did in his life. This missionary is well known and travels extensively, sharing about the amazing things God does through his ministry. One of his stories is of a time when he went to a church and the host greeted him with a welcome, thanking the missionary for coming back, and then raving about the last time the missionary had visited this church and how impacting it was. The missionary thought to himself, "*I've never been to this church before.*" He chalked it up as the host confusing him with another guest speaker. He then traveled to another city where the host pastor greeted him with a welcome, and thanked him for coming back, raving about the time he had visited this church last, and how impacting it was. The host added, "the song that you introduced was such a blessing…". The missionary said to this host, "I apologize, but this is my first visit to this church." The host pastor took out his phone and showed this missionary a video of the missionary himself singing and playing guitar at this church. The missionary also has documented evidence that he was actually in another city at the time of this previous visit to this church. What the Lord was showing him through this situation was that God was using him in multiple places at the same time. When I first heard this story, I thought to myself, *"Ok, maybe the missionary is missing some facts here. This is pretty wild."* But then the Lord spoke to me that we have no previous context for what Jesus described as "greater miracles." Jesus says in the Gospel of John, chapter 14:

> **12** *"I tell you this timeless truth: The person who follows me in faith, believing in me, will do the same mighty miracles that I do—even greater miracles than these because I go to be with my Father!*

Jesus left "greater miracles" completely undefined. In other words, God is free to do anything He wants to do, whether it violates your understanding or not. God is sovereign, and with Him all things are possible.

Let's look back at the Gospel of John, chapter 3, verse 2: Nicodemus begins, *"Master, we know that you are a teacher…"* The word 'know' is the same word Jesus uses when he says, *"Before a person can PERCEIVE …"* In other words, Jesus is not just trying to get Nicodemus to observe something, he is extending an invitation to *experience* the things—supernatural things—which he has seen.

I submit to you that whenever we place limits on God, we make our mind an idol, convincing ourselves we know more than God does or that our understanding is greater than God's.

In 2004, a friend of mine invited me to a meeting at a church about 2 hours away, where he was going to hear another friend of his from New Zealand minister as a guest speaker. I was reluctant, but I went because of our friendship. When we arrived, the gentleman was speaking; and he continued long enough that I felt I needed to get back to my family. My friend insisted that I wait a few minutes to allow this gentleman from New Zealand to pray for me. I did, and the gentleman prayed. As he did, he began to tell me with specifics about some things that had gone on in my life relationally, things that were emotionally challenging to me. He had my attention.

He then began to tell me that the Lord was saying He was sending my wife and me to the nations, and that He was sending us to nations where there was much poverty. He ended by saying in a prophetic commission to "Go. Go to nations."

My wife and I had been members of a church that had a strong international missions vision, so with the accuracy of the first part of the prophetic word, and the second part lining up with what was already in our hearts, I knew this was God. I went home and told my wife about this word. We prayed, "Okay, Lord. We know you're saying go to the nations, but where?" We prayed about it and were sensing Africa. Not long after, we were hosting a home group, and there was a newcomer who knew nothing about us, our church, or what we were praying at the time. At the end of the meeting, she stayed behind and shared with us that, in her heart, she saw Robin and me involved in missions in Africa.

That was confirmation enough for us. We then began to explore ways to get plugged into a ministry that had a presence on that continent. During that season, a neighbor friend, who happened to be a pastor and was from Kenya, Africa, crossed paths with me as we were walking into our homes. He invited me over for a spontaneous visit for tea. As we sat together, he began to tell me about how, by faith, the Lord brought him and his wife to the U.S. from Kenya. He came only knowing one contact, and with no money beyond his flight purchase. Doors began to open for him, and he has planted churches here in the U.S.

As he was telling me his story, I felt the Lord beginning to inspire me about what He had spoken to Robin and me about going to Africa. I mentioned to my neighbor friend how ironic it was that the Lord had sent him here to the U.S., because the Lord was now sending us to Africa. My friend responded with, "If you would like to go to Africa, I can make arrangements for you."

My wife and I prayed about this opportunity and felt it was from God. We accepted the offer; and my neighbor friend, whose name is Stanley, connected us with his family back in Kenya, who made preparations for our arrival. We knew we wanted to connect with an effort to help children and with a church that was doing outreach sharing the gospel. We arrived on a Wednesday and explained to our hosts, the extended family of our neighbor Stanley, what our interests were. They told us that sounded okay and that they would connect us with their pastor on Sunday. Well, it was Wednesday, and we were in a country we had never been in, with people we had never met. What were we to do for the next 4 days without a specific ministry agenda?

We decided, because we were staying for three weeks, to get some of the things we needed to make our stay comfortable. To start, we needed a power conversion adapter, and so we went to a local electronics store to purchase one. When we pulled into the parking lot and got out, we were greeted by a man who had a paralyzed hand. It was visibly charred, and it was paralyzed in an open hand position, asking us for a handout. I knew the Lord wanted us to pray for him, and so we did. The man gained functionality in his hand, and so was able to hold things in it, whereas before he could not.

This was the first of many healings that took place on this trip. We were walking through a congested area when we came across a man who walked with a cane. After prayer, he walked away carrying his cane. There were other healings that took place as well, and then the Lord began to speak to us of how Jesus walked. Jesus didn't wait for some ministry opportunity to release the kingdom. Twenty-four hours a day, seven days a week, Jesus was who Jesus was. He didn't need a platform to follow the Holy Spirit. So even if the path to your dream doesn't look like what you expected, you can always trust the Lord is doing something and we only need to tap into what His heart is in that moment.

Gathering with these mighty ones.

Cool cats.

CHAPTER 11
Desire of Nations

As time went on, a relationship developed with our friends in Kenya; and we began working alongside them in different ministry opportunities. The Lord then led us to start our nonprofit ministry called *Desire of Nations*, a name which comes from the book of Haggai, chapter 2:

> **1** *In the seventh month, in the one and twentieth day of the month, came the word of the Lord by the prophet Haggai, saying,* **2** *Speak now to Zerubbabel the son of Shealtiel, governor of Judah, and to Joshua the son of Josedech, the high priest, and to the residue of the people, saying,* **3** *Who is left among you that saw this house in her first glory? And how do ye see it now? Is it not in your eyes in comparison of it as nothing?* **4** *Yet now be strong, O Zerubbabel, saith the Lord; and be strong, O Joshua, son of Josedech, the high priest; and be strong, all ye people of the*

land, saith the Lord, and work: for I am with you, saith the Lord of hosts: **5** *According to the word that I covenanted with you when ye came out of Egypt, so my spirit remaineth among you: fear ye not.* **6** *For thus saith the Lord of hosts; Yet once, it is a little while, and I will shake the heavens, and the earth, and the sea, and the dry land;* **7** *And I will shake all nations, and the desire of all nations shall come: and I will fill this house with glory, saith the Lord of hosts.* **8** *The silver is mine, and the gold is mine, saith the Lord of hosts.* **9** *The glory of this latter house shall be greater than of the former, saith the Lord of hosts: and in this place will I give peace, saith the Lord of hosts.* (KJV)

It says in verse 7, *"…the desire of all nations shall come."* Then, in verse 8, *"The silver is mine and the gold is mine…."* There are a couple of beliefs concerning what is meant in verse 7 by *"the desire of all nations."* Some say it is metaphorically speaking of Jesus, who *is* the desire of all nations. Others say it means the valuable, precious stones, gems, gold, silver, etc. We say both. There are many places in the Bible where symbolism is used to describe Jesus. He is the lily of the valley, bright and morning star, Lion of the tribe of Judah, stone which the builders rejected, etc. So, it is all about Jesus. What is being talked about in this passage in chapter 2 is the rebuilding of the temple. God is telling them that He is going to provide what is necessary for the rebuilding: Jesus, (prophetically speaking), and the silver and the gold. It also says in the book of 1 Peter, chapter 2:

2 *In the same way that nursing infants cry for milk, you must intensely crave the pure spiritual milk of*

God's Word. For this "milk" will cause you to grow into maturity, fully nourished and strong for life 3 especially now that you have had a taste of the goodness of the Lord Jehovah and have experienced his kindness. 4 So keep coming to him who is the Living Stone though he was rejected and discarded by men but chosen by God and is priceless in God's sight. 5 Come and be his "living stones" who are continually being assembled into a sanctuary for God. For now you serve as holy priests, offering up spiritual sacrifices that he readily accepts through Jesus Christ.

The Lord asked my wife and me a question about where the most precious stones in the world are found. They are found underground in caves and in desolate places of the world, places where most people don't want to go. So, He told us, "That is where I want you to go, into these desolate places; and pull out these precious gems, with whom I want to decorate my Spiritual house that I am building." Hence the name *Desire of Nations*. We want to see them shine for His glory.

My wife came home from the video store, back when those existed, with a video based on a true story about the "lost boys of Sudan". In the 1980's and 90's, there was civil war in Sudan between the north and the south. The south suffered tremendous atrocities and, as a result, thousands of young boys fled the nation because of the death of their parents. They walked 1000 miles across the desert and ended up in refugee camps in other nations, one of those nations being Kenya. When the U.S. and the U.N. were made aware of the plight of these boys, they initiated a program to allow a number of these boys to resettle in the U.S. The documentary my wife brought home was based on a few of them.

One of the boys, who happens to be a Christian and who shares publicly about the things of God, is the primary figure in the documentary. Because of this, he became very well known. He has been on talk shows and has begun his own organizations. He became a voice of advocacy related to the atrocities that take place in Sudan. Through the media, he gained an audience of millions. After we viewed this video, the Lord challenged us with this boy's story, saying to us that if He can take someone like this boy, who has come from walking across the desert with barely a shirt on his back, (also having to eat things to survive that I am ashamed to state), and put him before an audience of millions, what is the potential of the lives of those He is sending us to?

After that, we began seeing these children in a whole new way. And now, not only are we reaching out to these children to give them help, but we will also see these children raised up as champions in the world; and we are in partnership with the Lord for this vision, this dream. I believe we all we need to see children in a way that moves us to partner in their destiny in this world.

The book of Jeremiah, chapter 1, verse 5, tells us that God has plans for us before we are born, even before we are conceived:

> **5** *"I knew you before I formed you in your mother's womb. Before you were born I set you apart...."* (NLT)

So, in scripture, when the Lord spoke to someone regarding their children, He did not talk to them about how cute or cuddly they were. He did not tell them what their child would weigh or what their length would be at birth. You see, God saw beyond all those things; and He spoke to parents about the child's destiny.

And He spoke of these things to some of these parents even before the child was conceived. This was true for Zechariah and Elizabeth; for Joseph and Mary; for Manoah, Samson's father, and his wife; etc.

What did the Lord say about these children? Well, in the example of Isaac and Rebecca, the Lord said to Rebecca, when she inquired as to why there was turmoil in her womb during her pregnancy:

> **Genesis 25:23** *And the Lord told her, "The sons in your womb will become two nations. From the very beginning, the two nations will be rivals. One nation will be stronger than the other; and your older son will serve your younger son."* (NLT)

The Lord called the fetuses "*nations.*" The plans He has for us don't just begin when we are born. They are well thought out, well planned, and even executed with detailed attention. The Lord spoke of John the Baptist's purpose prophetically before he was conceived, as He also did for others. So, how do we need to view children's ministry?

I believe we need to examine any thoughts of simply taking care of their needs while the big people get fed the Word in another part of the building. I believe equipping them to impact the world within their unique purpose – God's purpose – is what we would do well to do.

In light of scripture, each generation is to prepare the way for the next. For example, in the book of Exodus, the first generation that Moses brought out of the land of Egypt did not acquire that land God had called them into. It was the next generation that had to fight for it. Therefore, I submit that, in our generation, we are to gain ground for the kingdom so that the next generation can take the baton and run. As in a relay race, we can position them to inherit faith for things beyond those we had to contend for. We have to believe that each of us, and each generation, has been born for the time to which we were given. We are born to run our race well; and we are called to raise those children He entrusts to us in His nurture and admonition, so they might go beyond our leg of the race, even into that land flowing with milk and honey.

In the book of Hebrews, chapter 11, it says:

> **33** *Through faith's power they conquered kingdoms and established true justice. Their faith fastened onto their promises and pulled them into reality! It was faith that shut the mouth of lions,* **34** *put out the power of raging fire, and caused many to escape certain death by the sword. In their weakness their faith imparted power to make them strong! Faith sparked courage within them and they became mighty warriors in battle, pulling armies from another realm into battle array.* **35** *Faith-filled women saw their dead children raised in resurrection power. Yet it was faith that enabled others to endure great atrocities. They were stretched out on the wheel and tortured, and didn't deny their faith in order to be freed, because they longed for a more honorable and glorious resurrection!* **36** *Others were mocked and experienced the most severe beating with whips; they were in chains and imprisoned.* **37** *Some of these faith champions were brutally killed by stoning, being sawn in two or slaughtered by the sword. These lived in faith as they went about wearing goatskins*

and sheepskins for clothing. They lost everything they possessed, they endured great afflictions, and they were cruelly mistreated. **38** *They wandered the earth living in the desert wilderness, in caves, on barren mountains and in holes in the earth. Truly, the world was not even worthy of them, not realizing who they were.* **39** *These were the true heroes, commended for their faith, yet they lived in hope without receiving the fullness of what was promised them.*

This text talks about all those who have gone before us, whose faith fastened to promises, shut the mouths of lions, etc. It tells of others who suffered tremendous abuse, having not obtained the promise, because God would not let them come to all He had for them without us.

In a relay race, where the first man to run doesn't get to celebrate until the last man crosses the finish line, it is to the benefit of the man running the first leg to position the others to their best advantage. In scripture, that first generation coming out of Egypt is used as an example of those not to emulate. Can you imagine the fruit – or lack of fruit—if their testimony of faith was that which we should follow?

As in Hebrews 11, then, it is seen that those who come after us benefit from our pursuit, by faith, of all that God has for us: our dreams.

Meeting new friends in Oitao Preto.

CHAPTER 12
"LOL"

A friend said to me, "If what God has promised you isn't laughable, it probably isn't really from God." What did she mean? She meant that if your promise from Him isn't so outlandish that you can barely get your mind around how in the world it can happen, then it's probably not from Him. If you've laughed at your promise from God—like Sarah, Abraham's wife—don't worry, you're in good company. Sarah gets a lot of press for her laughing at the promise of God, but many don't take note of the fact that Abraham, our father of faith, actually laughed himself. In the book of Genesis, chapter 17, it says:

> **1** *When Abram was ninety-nine years old, the Lord appeared to him and said, "I am El-Shaddai—'God Almighty.' Serve me faithfully and live a blameless life.* **2** *I will make a covenant with you, by which I will guarantee to give you countless descendants."* **3** *At this, Abram fell face down on the ground.*

Then God said to him, 4 "This is my covenant with you: I will make you the father of a multitude of nations! 5 What's more, I am changing your name. It will no longer be Abram. Instead, you will be called Abraham, for you will be the father of many nations. 6 I will make you extremely fruitful. Your descendants will become many nations, and kings will be among them! 7 "I will confirm my covenant with you and your descendants after you, from generation to generation. This is the everlasting covenant: I will always be your God and the God of your descendants after you. 8 And I will give the entire land of Canaan, where you now live as a foreigner, to you and your descendants. It will be their possession forever, and I will be their God." 9 Then God said to Abraham, "Your responsibility is to obey the terms of the covenant. You and all your descendants have this continual responsibility. 10 This is the covenant that you and your descendants must keep: Each male among you must be circumcised. 11 You must cut off the flesh of your foreskin as a sign of the covenant between me and you. 12 From generation to generation, every male child must be circumcised on the eighth day after his birth. This applies not only to members of your family but also to the servants born in your household and the foreign-born servants whom you have purchased. 13 All must be circumcised. Your bodies will bear the mark of my everlasting covenant. 14 Any male who fails to be circumcised will be cut off from the covenant family for breaking the covenant." 15 Then God said to

Abraham, "Regarding Sarai, your wife—her name will no longer be Sarai. From now on her name will be Sarah. 16 And I will bless her and give you a son from her! Yes, I will bless her richly, and she will become the mother of many nations. Kings of nations will be among her descendants." 17 Then Abraham bowed down to the ground, but he laughed to himself in disbelief. "How could I become a father at the age of 100?" he thought. "And how can Sarah have a baby when she is ninety years old?" 18 So Abraham said to God, "May Ishmael live under your special blessing!" 19 But God replied, "No—Sarah, your wife, will give birth to a son for you. You will name him Isaac, and I will confirm my covenant with him and his descendants as an everlasting covenant. 20 As for Ishmael, I will bless him also, just as you have asked. I will make him extremely fruitful and multiply his descendants. He will become the father of twelve princes, and I will make him a great nation. 21 But my covenant will be confirmed with Isaac, who will be born to you and Sarah about this time next year." (NLT)

God gave Abraham this amazing promise; and it says in verse 17 that Abraham bowed to the ground and laughed at what God had to say. Abraham said, *"May Ishmael live under your special blessing!"*

What I like about this response from Abraham is that God saw it totally differently. It says of Abraham in the Epistle to the Romans, chapter 4:

18 Even when there was no reason for hope, Abraham

kept hoping—believing that he would become the father of many nations. For God had said to him, "That's how many descendants you will have!" **19** *And Abraham's faith did not weaken, even though, at about 100 years of age, he figured his body was as good as dead—and so was Sarah's womb.* **20** *Abraham never wavered in believing God's promise. In fact, his faith grew stronger, and in this he brought glory to God.* **21** *He was fully convinced that God is able to do whatever he promises.* **22** *And because of Abraham's faith, God counted him as righteous.* (NLT)

It says he considered not the condition of his own body, neither the condition of Sarah's womb. You see, when God writes your story, He is not looking at the things that we consider faults but sees the fact that you didn't give up, you didn't throw in the towel, you didn't curse God and die, etc. God sees you as a total victor. He's looking at the positives He has established in you and not your negatives.

I was taking my children to a children's meeting one evening, and my son asked me, "Dad, are you ready for the apocalypse?" The question kind of took me by surprise. He was maybe 9 or 10 years old. I didn't know he even knew what an apocalypse was. Anyhow, I said, "I hope so." Then, a couple of days later, I was studying the passage in Matthew where Jesus asks His disciples whom men were saying He, the Son of Man, was. It says in the Gospel of Matthew, chapter 16:

13 *When Jesus came to the region of Caesarea Philippi, he asked his disciples, "Who do people say that the Son of Man is?"* **14** *"Well," they replied, "some* *say John the Baptist, some say Elijah, and others say Jeremiah or one of the other prophets."* **15** *Then he asked them, "But who do you say I am?"* **16** *Simon Peter answered, "You are the Messiah, the Son of the living God."* **17** *Jesus replied, "You are blessed, Simon son of John, because my Father in heaven has revealed this to you. You did not learn this from any human being.* **18** *Now I say to you that you are Peter (which means 'rock'), and upon this rock I will build my church, and all the powers of hell will not conquer it.* **19** *And I will give you the keys of the Kingdom of Heaven. Whatever you forbid on earth will be forbidden in heaven, and whatever you permit on earth will be permitted in heaven."* **20** *Then he sternly warned the disciples not to tell anyone that he was the Messiah.* (NLT)

In verse 17, Jesus says a human being did not reveal to Peter who Jesus really was. Peter could see. He could see what the Father was showing him about who Jesus was.

As I studied this passage, I looked up what was meant by "*You did not learn...*" (verse 17) in Greek text, the original language the New Testament was written in. The word in the original language of the New Testament was *apokalyptō*. That is the Greek word for the English word *apocalypse*. I realized that the Lord was speaking to me through my son; He wanted to reveal something to me. In this passage, Jesus says to Peter, "*...I will give to you the keys of the kingdom of Heaven. Whatever you forbid on earth will be forbidden in heaven, and whatever you permit on earth will be permitted in heaven.*" In other words, "*Peter, I'm giving you authority to bind and loose according to what Heaven is doing, because you can see* *what is going on in Heaven. You have been receptive to what the Father is revealing. Therefore, you can partner with the Father to loose what is loosed in the Heavenly realm, and bind on earth what is bound in the Heavenly realm."*

And this is how Jesus walked. Read what He said in the Gospel of John, chapter 5:

> **19** *So Jesus said, "I speak to you timeless truth. The Son is not able to do anything from himself or through my own initiative. I only do the works that I see the Father doing, for the Son does the same works as his Father.*

Jesus also says in the Gospel of Matthew, chapter 16:

> **18** *I give you the name Peter, a stone. And this truth of who I am will be the bedrock foundation on which I will build my church—my legislative assembly, and the power of death will not be able to overpower it!*

In talking about the power of death, this is a place the enemy has disguised as a place with no hope. This could be a place in our lives, a city, a nation. These are places in which the enemy, speaking of Satan, or the demonic, has set up camp and tried to take ownership, attempting to determine who goes in and who goes out. Also, these places do not look easily penetrable at all, and this is why it is so important to *see*. Therefore, one must be available for Jesus to reveal what He has to say about a circumstance. To *see* things as Jesus sees them is the way to prevail over the power of death.

We all know that Jesus Himself builds His church, as He says in verse 18. But we can also recognize that, in this verse, He has included the church in the building process, as He says the power of death will not prevail against it (the church). God does use people to partner with Him in building. If the Lord is going after the gates of hell, how do we see the "hopeless situations?" How do we see those places where the enemy has said, "You can't come in here?" King David was one who could see as God saw.

> **2 Samuel 5:4** *David was thirty years old when he began to reign, and he reigned forty years in all.* **5** *He had reigned over Judah from Hebron for seven years and six months, and from Jerusalem he reigned over all Israel and Judah for thirty-three years.* **6** *David then led his men to Jerusalem to fight against the Jebusites, the original inhabitants of the land who were living there. The Jebusites taunted David, saying, "You'll never get in here! Even the blind and lame could keep you out!" For the Jebusites thought they were safe.* **7** *But David captured the fortress of Zion, which is now called the City of David.* (NLT)

No hesitancy. David just saw. He did it when he faced Goliath, and he did it when he advanced his kingdom. His information was from a Heavenly source. How do we see places like North Korea, places in the Middle East, China, etc? Are we seeing them as those who will be lovers of Jesus, to the point that we are willing to be a part, so that there is a conduit for it to be "on earth as it is in Heaven?" Those who build with the Lord and prevail against the gates will be those who can *see*. This can come down to the individual. What do we see in people who look like they're in rebellion to God, unholy, unrighteous, wicked, caught in all kinds of sin? What do we see? Peter saw who Jesus really is. We need to be able to see who Jesus really is, and we need to see who people really are. Can you see it before it looks like what it's supposed to on the outside? The builders with Jesus are seeing the nations transformed. What about our own lives? What are we seeing about the places where something has been a certain way our entire life, a place we've yet to experience breakthrough? "It's always been this way." How do you see it? The book of Isaiah, chapter 43, says:

> **19** *For I am about to do something new. See, I have already begun! Do you not see it? I will make a pathway through the wilderness. I will create rivers in the dry wasteland.* (NLT)

When Jesus asked in the Gospel of Matthew, chapter 16, verse 13, *"Who do people say that the Son of Man is?,"* it says that the disciples responded by saying that some were believing Jesus was John the Baptist reincarnate; some were saying Elijah; and some said Jesus was one of the old prophets. The people who were saying these things were getting their information from the wrong source. They had no context for what they were experiencing with Jesus doing what He was, so they filled in with what they already understood to some extent. Something they had experienced. Something familiar, as if to say, *"This can't be something new. You see, we have figured God out; and He does only what we know He will do. Therefore, if it doesn't fit into our box, it can't be God."* Because they had no context in which to place Him, they wrote Jesus off as less than God and then mentally filed what Jesus was doing under something God wasn't doing. After all, God does not come down to the earth in human flesh. Who ever heard of such a thing?

I'm telling you that God is going to do things in our day, something that we will miss if we don't get our information from the proper source. We could miss a move of God if we cannot *see,* because it may look totally different that any move we have seen before. We need to be in tune with what Heaven has to say. If we're going to build with Him, we're going to have to be able to recognize Jesus.

I once attended a meeting where God was moving powerfully. There were probably 10,000 people in this meeting, and there were expressions and manifestations of all kinds in response to what the Lord was doing. Because of this, it seemed as though what God was doing was very big. I felt so insignificant, and this made a cry come up in my heart: "Lord, I don't want to miss what you are doing!" The Lord responded to me, "If you don't want to miss what I am doing, you have to recognize one thing: that you don't know everything." He began to speak to me about the importance of coming to Him as a little child.

> **Mark 10:15** *Listen to the truth I speak: Whoever does not open their arms to receive God's kingdom like a teachable child will never enter it.*"

Kingdom life is relational. It's relational with God. I don't know how many questions my children asked me during their single digit childhood about what something is, what something means, why is this that way, how did this get to be? Our Heavenly Father wants us to approach Him as children who trust Him. It's not that we won't ever understand things; but in those places where we encounter things we don't understand, He wants us to walk with Him relationally. That is why the Pharisees, scribes, and Sadducees missed who Jesus was. Because without relationship, they couldn't get beyond what God had done before and believe He just might do something differently. They thought they had seen all of His character and capability, all of who He is and what He does, by their minute examination of the past; and they weren't open to dialogue with the Father about who Jesus is, like Peter was in the Gospel of Matthew, chapter 16, verses 13-17.

The Pharisees' view was a distant, judging determination to hold onto their own perspective; and that left no room for the new.

We can be similar sometimes. We say we want signs and wonders; but, really, we only want signs, because we don't like to not understand what is happening or what God is doing. Wonders have no answer because they are out of the scope of our current understanding. And when we have no answer, we tend to file things in the wrong place in our minds. We do not realize we must allow God to make a new file, as it were. God's intent is that we, like Peter, interact with the things of God relationally and get our understanding from Him.

Peter's open heart to God brought him to see, and then say, *"You are the Messiah, the Son of the living God."*

CHAPTER 13
True Friendship

When God told Moses to build the tabernacle, it says in the book of Exodus, chapter 25:

> **8** *"Have the people of Israel build me a holy sanctuary so I can live among them.* **9** *You must build this Tabernacle and its furnishings exactly according to the pattern I will show you.* (NLT)

In building, Moses was shown; and he *saw.* In the same way, God is building His church. God told Moses the tabernacle was to be made according to what was shown to him. That is how we are to participate in building with Jesus. This endeavor is about friendship and intimacy. The Bible talks about us—as the church—being the Bride of Christ. It says in the Epistle to the Ephesians, in chapter 5:

> **30** *He serves and satisfies us as members of his body.*
> **31** *For this reason a man is to leave his father and*

*his mother and lovingly hold to his wife, since the two have become joined as one flesh. **32** Marriage is the beautiful design of the Almighty, a great and sacred mystery—meant to be a vivid example of Christ and his church.*

We are Jesus' Bride; but in addition to that, I believe Jesus wants a Bride who is a friend. How many of us have gone into a restaurant where we saw an older couple sitting together and barely speaking to each other? They said maybe, "Can you pass the salt?" or "May I use that ketchup?" But the atmosphere of their time with one another was dry and void of real connection. That is positional function and role fulfillment, but it is without intimacy. Well, God doesn't want that. How many of us have gone to a restaurant and seen a couple enjoying each other's company so much that it's kind of mushy, obnoxious, silly, googly-eyed, craziness? They are lovers as well as friends. God wants that.

It says in the Gospel of Matthew, in chapter 25:

34 *Then the King will turn to those on his right and say, 'You have a special place in my Father's heart. Come and experience the full inheritance of the kingdom realm that has been destined for you from before the foundation of the world!* **35** *For when you saw me hungry, you fed me. When you found me thirsty, you gave me something to drink. When I had no place to stay, you invited me in,* **36** *and when I was poorly clothed, you covered me. When I was sick, you tenderly cared for me, and when I was in prison you visited me.'*

What is described in these verses is going to happen because

Jesus said it would. It is great. It is awesome. It's to be celebrated. Also, I believe for some, what will happen is in the Gospel of John, chapter 15:

> **15** *I have never called you 'servants,' because a master doesn't confide in his servants, and servants don't always understand what the master is doing. But I call you my most intimate friends, for I reveal to you everything that I've heard from my Father.*

This is how Jesus walked with the Father and is the ultimate picture of intimacy. And in intimacy, we hear Him sharing His heart. God likes to share His thoughts; and if you're willing to hear, He just might ask you to participate with Him in something the world has never seen before. It's true! Heaven was so bursting with the announcement of what Jesus came to do that it was communicated through angels in the Gospel of Luke, chapter 2:

> **8** *That night, in a field near Bethlehem, there were shepherds watching over their flocks.* **9** *Suddenly, an angel of the Lord appeared in radiant splendor before them, lighting up the field with the blazing glory of God, and the shepherds were terrified!* **10** *But the angel reassured them, saying, "Don't be afraid. For I have come to bring you good news, the most joyous news the world has ever heard! And it is for everyone everywhere!* **11** *For today in Bethlehem a rescuer was born for you. He is the Lord Yahweh, the Messiah.* **12** *You will recognize him by this miracle sign: You will find a baby wrapped in strips of cloth and lying in a feeding trough!"* **13** *Then all at once, a vast number of glorious angels appeared,*

> *the very armies of heaven! And they all praised God,*
> *singing:* **14** *"Glory to God in the highest realms of*
> *heaven! For there is peace and a good hope given to*
> *the sons of men."*

His desire to communicate was demonstrated through a star in the Gospel of Matthew, chapter 2:

> **2** *and inquired of the people, "Where is the child*
> *who is born king of the Jewish people? We observed*
> *his star rising in the sky and we've come to bow before*
> *him in worship."*

Even Caiaphas, the High Priest, who couldn't recognize Jesus was the Messiah, prophesied about the death of Jesus, who would die for that nation, in the Gospel of John, chapter 11:

> **49** *Now Caiaphas, the high priest that year, spoke*
> *up and said, "You don't understand a thing!* **50**
> *Don't you realize we'd be much better off if this one*
> *man were to die for the people than for the whole*
> *nation to perish?"* **51** *(This prophecy that Jesus was*
> *destined to die for the Jewish people didn't come*
> *from Caiaphas himself, but he was moved by God*
> *to prophesy as the chief priest.*

Along with so many other references in scripture, this tells us that God wants to share things with us. Jesus talked multiple times about having ears to hear; so, it is not a matter of God not speaking, but of our need to have the willingness – or childlike desire – to hear. It's just a matter of listening.

Sometimes we can approach God with a "maybe He'll throw

IT'S SUPPOSED TO BE *IMPOSSIBLE*

me a bone" type of mentality. In the Gospel of Mark, chapter 1, it says:

> **40** *On one occasion, a leper came and threw himself down in front of Jesus, pleading for his healing, saying, "You have the power to heal me right now if only you really want to!"* **41** *Being deeply moved with tender compassion, Jesus reached out and touched the skin of the leper and told him, "Of Course I want you to be healed—so now, be cleansed!"* **42** *Instantly his leprous sores completely disappeared and his skin became smooth!*

In this passage we can see that the leper approached Jesus with a question of whether or not Jesus cared about his circumstance. Because of the traditional treatment of his condition, he might have felt he deserved no favor and, therefore, might not be heard. We can often feel as though Jesus has favorites. I have heard it said about the apostle John, that He was the closest to Jesus of all the apostles. We take this from passages like:

> **Matthew 17:1** *Six days later Jesus took Peter and the two brothers, James and John, and led them up a high mountain to be alone.* (NLT)

> **Mark 5:37** *Then Jesus stopped the crowd and wouldn't let anyone go with him except Peter, James, and John (the brother of James).* (NLT)

> **John 13:20** *I tell you the truth, anyone who welcomes my messenger is welcoming me, and anyone who welcomes me is welcoming the Father who sent*

> *me."* **21** *Now Jesus was deeply troubled, and he ex-*
> *claimed, "I tell you the truth, one of you will betray*
> *me!"* **22** *The disciples looked at each other, wondering*
> *whom he could mean.* **23** *The disciple Jesus loved*
> *was sitting next to Jesus at the table.* **24** *Simon Peter*
> *motioned to him to ask, "Who's he talking about?"*
> **25** *So that disciple leaned over to Jesus and asked,*
> *"Lord, who is it?"* **26** *Jesus responded, "It is the one*
> *to whom I give the bread I dip in the bowl." And*
> *when he had dipped it, he gave it to Judas, son of*
> *Simon Iscariot.* (NLT)

When the apostles were together with Jesus during the last supper meal, when Jesus told them one of them would betray Him, John was the one Peter asked to get the inside scoop from Jesus. He was sitting closest to Jesus. In fact, the King James Version says, in verse 25, that John was even lying on Jesus's breast. This is a place of closeness. It is wonderful that John felt so loved by Jesus that he would take it upon himself to be in such an unreserved posture with Jesus. This is close friendship. However, I would like to submit to you that Jesus's breast did not have a sign on it that said, "reserved for John only". Any one of the disciples could have taken that posture with Jesus. John believed and received the love that Jesus had for him and he acted accordingly. I believe this is why John was able to pen what is called *the epistle of love*, formally titled The First Epistle of John. In this book, John speaks thoroughly on love, as one who is familiar with it by experience. I quote him:

> **1 John 3:1** *Look with wonder at the depth of the*
> *Father's marvelous love that he has lavished on us!*
> *He has called us and made us his very own beloved*

children. …

John received Jesus's love and acted on it. Do you believe Jesus loves you? Are you acting like it? Are you positioning yourself like John did? Are you expecting that He will speak to you about things that He hasn't spoken to anyone else about?

That's one of the things that breakthrough people do. They hear from God things that are specific solutions to advance the kingdom of God in our world. They hear because they position themselves close to Him. They love Him lavishly because they know that is how He loves them.

Lavishly: that is how He loves us. We have only to look at the cross to see it. Once we really know that, there will be no question in our hearts that we belong right there next to Him, listening. If self-consciousness keeps us back, if we consider our own merits, it is because we have not been focusing on *His* merits. After all, it is not what we can do – it is what He did and does.

We all have to get past what we have and don't have. It says in the Gospel of Matthew, chapter 12:

> **1** *One Saturday, on the day of rest, Jesus and his disciples were walking through a field of wheat. The disciples were hungry, so they plucked off some heads of grain and rubbed them in their hands to eat.* **2** *But when some of the Pharisees saw what was happening, they said to him, "Look! Your disciples shouldn't be harvesting grain on the Sabbath!"* **3** *Jesus responded, "Haven't you ever read what King David and his men did when they were hungry?* **4** *They entered the house of God and ate the sacred bread of God's presence, violating the law by eating bread that only the priests were allowed to eat.* **5**

"And haven't you read in the Torah that the priests violated the rules of the Sabbath by carrying out their duties in the temple on a Saturday, and yet they are without blame? 6 But I say to you, there is one here who is even greater than the temple. 7 If only you could learn the meaning of the words 'I want compassion more than a sacrifice,' you wouldn't be condemning my innocent disciples. 8 For the Son of Man exercises his lordship over the Sabbath."

I find it interesting that, in this passage, it never occurred to the disciples who were walking with Jesus that what they were doing could be something that was violating the law. They had to have been somewhat conscience of the law. Of course, they were not as knowledgeable as a Pharisee or a Sadducee; but they were at least aware of such common things. They did know that the Messiah was coming. We can give them that. I would guess they knew a bit more as well. It says in the Gospel of John, chapter 2:

12 After this, Jesus, his mother and brothers and his disciples went to Capernaum and stayed there for a few days. 13 But the time was close for the Jewish Passover to begin, so Jesus walked to Jerusalem. 14 As he went into the temple courtyard, he noticed it was filled with merchants selling oxen, lambs, and doves for exorbitant prices, while others were over-charging as they exchanged currency behind their counters. 15 So Jesus found some rope and made it into a whip. Then he drove out every one of them and their animals from the courtyard of the temple, and he kicked over their tables filled with money, scattering it everywhere! 16 And he shouted at the

IT'S SUPPOSED TO BE *IMPOSSIBLE*

merchants, "Get these things out of here! Don't you dare make my Father's house into a center for merchandise!" **17** *That's when his disciples remembered the Scripture: "I am consumed with a fiery passion to keep your house pure!"*

How is it that the disciples, being less formally educated, were more educated on what God's heart was in that circumstance than those who had studied for years to attain to what the disciples were displaying? Because the disciples didn't rely on what they had (their level of education related to God), but on what was available to them in relationship with Jesus.

They had read some of the scriptures; but it didn't occur to them, on this occasion, that there was anything wrong with what they were doing. The Pharisees, on the other hand, were completely conscious of what was allowed and not allowed at all times. The disciples knew they were accepted by God. The Pharisees were trying their best to *become* acceptable to God. The disciples were in tune with God's heart in this circumstance. The Pharisees couldn't see God's heart.

Often, in our approach to what God has called us to, we can base our response on the formula that the Pharisees in this passage used. How much money do I have so that I might fulfill what He has called me to? How much talent, if any, do I have? How equipped am I in this certain area of my calling? Often, we begin by judging our qualifications based on the results of this type of self-assessment. Even a seasoned believer might tend to base their qualifications on what they have to offer rather than what God is showing them. "Let's see, I've gained an education; I know the scriptures; I know the history of how God worked among His people; I know the things God said in scripture to

113

people; therefore, I know how God speaks." It says of Moses in the book of Acts, chapter 7:

> **21** *so they had to abandon him to his fate. But God arranged that Pharaoh's daughter would find him, take him home, and raise him as her own son.* **22** *So Moses was fully trained in the royal courts and educated in the highest wisdom Egypt had to offer, until he arose as a powerful prince and an eloquent orator.*

Even though he was trained and educated and *"a powerful prince and an eloquent orator,"* Moses could never have fulfilled what God had purposed over him with just his natural skills. While he was mighty in word and deed, as a man he was limited; and it wasn't enough. God had to allow Moses to come to a place where he knew what he had was not enough, so that he would rely on God and what God added to the equation. The story is summarized in the following passages:

> **Acts 7:30** *After forty years had passed, while he was in the desert near Mount Sinai, the Messenger of Yahweh appeared to him in the midst of a flaming thorn bush.*

> **Exodus 3:10** *Now go, for I am sending you to Pharaoh. You must lead my people Israel out of Egypt."* **11** *But Moses protested to God, "Who am I to appear before Pharaoh? Who am I to lead the people of Israel out of Egypt?"* **12** *God answered, "I will be with you.* (NLT)

Exodus 4:1 *But Moses protested again, "What if they won't believe me or listen to me? What if they say, 'The Lord never appeared to you'?" **2** Then the Lord asked him, "What is that in your hand?" "A shepherd's staff," Moses replied. **3** "Throw it down on the ground," the Lord told him. So Moses threw down the staff, and it turned into a snake! Moses jumped back. **4** Then the Lord told him, "Reach out and grab its tail." So Moses reached out and grabbed it, and it turned back into a shepherd's staff in his hand. **5** "Perform this sign," the Lord told him. "Then they will believe that the Lord, the God of their ancestors—the God of Abraham, the God of Isaac, and the God of Jacob—really has appeared to you." **6** Then the Lord said to Moses, "Now put your hand inside your cloak." So Moses put his hand inside his cloak, and when he took it out again, his hand was white as snow with a severe skin disease. **7** "Now put your hand back into your cloak," the Lord said. So Moses put his hand back in, and when he took it out again, it was as healthy as the rest of his body. **8** The Lord said to Moses, "If they do not believe you and are not convinced by the first miraculous sign, they will be convinced by the second sign. **9** And if they don't believe you or listen to you even after these two signs, then take some water from the Nile River and pour it out on the dry ground. When you do, the water from the Nile will turn to blood on the ground." **10** But Moses pleaded with the Lord, "O Lord, I'm not very good with words. I never have been, and I'm not now, even though* *you have spoken to me. I get tongue-tied, and my words get tangled."* **11** *Then the Lord asked Moses, "Who makes a person's mouth? Who decides whether people speak or do not speak, hear or do not hear, see or do not see? Is it not I, the Lord?* **12** *Now go! I will be with you as you speak, and I will instruct you in what to say."* (NLT)

So, if I don't have any talent, any money, or any qualifications, am I better off? No, that isn't the answer, either. God has factored Himself into the purpose and the calling that he has over our lives. That is why sometimes we don't have what we think we need in the natural, because God is not worried about those things. Moses still thought being mighty in word and deed was the answer. God was communicating to him that it didn't matter. We can be in the same place sometimes when we place limitations on what God can do through us according to what we do or do not possess in and of ourselves, whether that be education and intelligence, possessions, resources, finances, level of influence, etc. Moses was called to be with God and to do what he was called to do *with* God. What Moses did was meant, then, to be from that place of being with God, in relationship, always.

As Jesus said when He commissioned the disciples in the Gospel of Matthew, chapter 28:

> **19** *Now go in my authority and make disciples of all nations, baptizing them in the name of the Father, the Son, and the Holy Spirit.* **20** *And teach them to faithfully follow all that I have commanded you. And never forget that I am with you every day, even to the completion of this age."*

Moses said, "*I cannot talk*." When he could talk, it wasn't enough. Being able to talk had nothing to do with it. There was still a residue of the mindset that, if he possessed that talent, it would be enough. Moses' being articulate could never have turned the waters of the Nile River into blood, brought massive amounts of frogs up onto the land, turned dust into lice, brought sickness upon the cattle, inflicted the Egyptians with boils, brought hail of fire and brimstone down, brought a huge mass of locusts to the land, brought darkness for days upon the land of Egypt (except where the children of Israel were dwelling), killed the firstborn of every Egyptian, nor opened up the Red Sea so that the children of Israel could walk through it on dry ground, and so on.

Pharaoh would hardly let the people go, even as mighty as these acts of God were. How much less would have been produced based on the level of articulation of a man's speech?

At that time, Moses was still placing natural limitations above God, as we all do at times. Moses didn't realize how high God had called him. He had no idea of the great things that God intended for him and how committed God was to fulfill that calling. He thought that God was only able to call him as high as his natural talent could take him. But God had called him higher. He has called you higher. You are called to something higher than what can be produced by natural means. If you see only your earthly limitations, you will not fully achieve His plan for your life.

This is why the Apostle Paul could say in the Epistle to the Philippians, Chapter 3:

> **12** *I admit that I haven't yet acquired the absolute*
> *fullness that I'm pursuing, but I run with passion*

into his abundance so that I may reach the purpose that Jesus Christ has called me to fulfill and wants me to discover. 13 I don't depend on my own strength to accomplish this;

Paul also says in the Epistle to the Philippians, chapter 4:

12–13 *I know what it means to lack, and I know what it means to experience overwhelming abundance. For I'm trained in the secret of overcoming all things, whether in fullness or in hunger. And I find that the strength of Christ's explosive power infuses me to conquer every difficulty.*

Paul learned that God was His source for all things. He was not wearied if he had, and he was not concerned if he didn't have. He could deal with every situation through Jesus who was his strength.

What are you looking at in your life that you feel qualifies or disqualifies you for what God has for your life? None of it does. Jesus is, and always will be, the only thing that qualifies us for anything in God.

CHAPTER 14

Recognizing the Good God Has Placed in Others

God has given us great people placed in and around our lives as an inspiration. These are people who are from all walks of life and who hold different positions relationally to us. Parents are a huge influence. Other family members, friends, colleagues, associates, etc., can all inspire us – in many ways. These can be people who have accomplished great things. They can even be people we don't know or we know from afar. They can be celebrities, world leaders, etc.

We want to gain the inspiration that God intended from these people, because it can have a major impact on our lives in a great way. We would do well to never underestimate or minimize the impact an individual can have in our lives. I am not talking about dependency, but only to recognize the good things in other people; this can be a very positive thing for us. This is true even if we feel as though a particular person, or "type" of person, could never have anything to offer us.

There is a story Jesus told in the Gospel of Matthew, chapter 21:

> **23** *After this Jesus went into the temple courts and taught the people. The leading priests and Jewish elders approached him and interrupted him and asked, "By what power do you do these things, and who granted you the authority to teach here?"* **24** *Jesus answered them, "I too have a question to ask you. If you can answer this question, then I will tell you by what power I do these things.* **25** *From where did John's authority to baptize come from? From heaven or from people?"* **26** *They stepped away and debated among themselves, saying, "How should we answer this? If we say from heaven, he will say to us, 'Then why didn't you respond to John and believe what he said?' But if we deny that God gave him his authority, we'll be mobbed by the people, for they're convinced that John was God's prophet."* **27** *So they finally answered, "We don't know." "Then neither will I tell you from where my power comes to do these things!" he replied. The Parable of Two Sons* **28** *Jesus said to his critics, "Tell me what you think of this parable: "There once was a man with two sons. The father came to the first and said, 'Son, I want you to go and work in the vineyard today.'* **29** *The son replied, 'I'd rather not.' But afterward, he deeply regretted what he said to his father, changed his mind, and decided to go to the vineyard.* **30** *The father approached the second son and said the same*

*thing to him. The son replied, 'Father, I will go and do as you said.' But he never did—he didn't go to the vineyard. **31** Tell me now, which of these two sons did the will of his father?" They answered him, "The first one." Jesus said, "You're right. For many sinners, tax collectors, and prostitutes are going into God's kingdom realm ahead of you! **32** John came to show you the path of goodness and righteousness, yet the despised and outcasts believed in him, but you did not. When you saw them turn, you neither repented of your ways nor believed his words."*

In verse 32, Jesus says to the Pharisees that the sinners, tax collectors, and prostitutes believed John, whereas the Pharisees did not; they did not repent after seeing it. The Pharisees considered sinners, tax collectors, and prostitutes to be outcasts, of no significance in life to them at all. Jesus is telling them that certainly, if the least repented at John's warning, the leaders who prided themselves on discerning the scriptures should have been first—before those—to repent.

In other words, *you should have paid attention to what you saw the sinners, tax collectors, and prostitutes doing, and you should have let their example motivate you.* This must have stopped them cold. What an insult. *"You mean THEY, were an example to US?"*

Yes. It is so important that we never minimize others but remember that every living person was created by God, who does all things well and for His pleasure. Each person holds a very significant place in the heart of God. We never know who God might want to use as an inspiration to us or others. Often, and I dare say, very often, God chooses many whom we would never expect. It is to our benefit to recognize the value on every human life and honor that. Each is priceless. There is no higher price that Heaven could have paid than it did for every individual who has and who will ever exist in our world. The blood of Jesus has no comparison.

There is a passage in the Gospel of Mark, chapter 14, where it says:

> **1** *Two days before the Passover and the Feast of Unleavened Bread, the leading priests and religious scholars were committed to finding a way to secretly arrest Jesus and have him executed.* **2** *But they all agreed that their plot could not succeed if they carried it out during the days of the feast, for they said, "There could be a riot among the people."* **3** *Now Jesus was in Bethany, in the home of Simon, a man Jesus had healed of leprosy. And as he was reclining at the table, a woman came into the house, holding an alabaster flask. It was filled with the highest quality of fragrant and expensive oil. She walked right up to Jesus, and with a gesture of extreme devotion, she broke the flask and poured out the precious oil over his head.* **4** *But some were highly indignant when they saw this, and they complained to one another, saying, "What a total waste!* **5** *It could have been sold for a great sum, and the money could have benefited the poor." So they scolded her harshly.* **6** *Jesus said to them, "Leave her alone! Why are you so critical of this woman? She has honored me with this beautiful act of kindness.* **7** *For you will always have the poor, whom you can help whenever you want, but you will not always have me.* **8** *When she*

poured the fragrant oil over me, she was preparing my body in advance of my burial. She has done all that she could to honor me. **9** *I promise you that as this wonderful gospel spreads all over the world, the story of her lavish devotion to me will be mentioned in memory of her."*

Here is an instance where a woman might be a church member but holds no position, no title. She may not even know many people in the church, but she loves God. She loves God in an amazing way, so much so that she wants to take a precious token and give it to Him in order to demonstrate her love for Him. It is something very valuable, very precious. So, she lavishes it on Him, and rightfully so; He is worthy.

It so happens, however, in this particular passage, that those who could have stood to gain from this example, and who I believe *could* have been an example of a right response to someone else's expression of unorthodox, unexpected, extravagant love, *instead* found themselves offended. They were expressing a kind of religion that said things should not be done like that.

These opinions echo down even today: *That is a different way to worship God. I don't like that worship song. All they do is ask for money. Why is the pastor wearing jeans? Why is that like this and why is this like that?*

Interestingly, the apostles, who were leaders of the church and who should have been those who affirmed what God was doing, actually resisted it.

But, oops…Jesus defended her.

I love what He said: *"I promise you that as this wonderful gospel spreads all over the world, the story of her lavish devotion to me will be mentioned in memory of her."*

He explained to them that this was not a small deal. Jesus said He had chosen to send the account of what she had done all around the world. He was telling them—and us—that this example of extravagant love for Him would be used to inspire others from that time forward.

Interestingly enough, Judas was just the opposite. Not only was he not giving extravagant love to Jesus, he was taking. Extravagant love is offensive to those who approach Jesus and the things of God with a "what's in it for me" mentality. These are more likely to say, *"What have you done for me lately? How is this affecting me?"* It's the same heart. That kind of thing is a normal bump in the road of maturity as we journey with God. We learn, as the apostles did. We see that all but Judas didn't stay in that place, and we don't need to either.

Why am I writing about this topic? Because breakthrough people often get resistance from different sources. It is good to note the resistance this woman was confronted by and that she didn't defend herself. She didn't come up with some passage of the scripture justifying why she was right. She just kept loving on Jesus, and He took care of it all.

This is a good example of how to deal with resistance of every kind. Just keep loving on Jesus. He will take care of you, just as He did with the woman in this passage. I am not saying that you ignore leadership. I am NOT saying that at all. On the contrary, honor and obey, and in that obedience, keep loving Jesus. It says in the Epistle to the Romans, in chapter 13:

> **1** *Every person must submit to and support the authorities over him. For there can be no authority in the universe except by God's appointment, which means that every authority that exists has been in-*

stituted by God. **2** *So to resist authority is to resist the divine order of God, which results in severe consequences.* **3** *For civil authorities don't intimidate those who are doing good, but those who are doing evil. So do what is right and you'll never need to fear those in authority. They will commend you for your good citizenship.*

You don't have to worry about whether or not you have favor with your leaders. God will take care of that. You only need to honor; respect; and, as God says in this passage, submit yourself to their leadership. God is sovereign and causes it all to work together for your good.

Some things we pursue or step out into will be from God and some things won't. That's a part of learning as we walk with God. Thank God for leaders who can help us with that. We have to be humble in the pursuit of our dreams. We can't just vaunt ourselves. The Lord spoke to my wife and me that our greatest effectiveness would come in partnership with the rest of the body of Christ. I believe that is why there is such power of God's influence so often seen in the Bible when His followers were in unity.

Friends in Brazil.

CHAPTER 15

We're in This Together

POWER IN UNITY

In the book of 2 Chronicles, chapter 5, we see a powerful example of God's response to the unity of the worshippers:

> **12** *And the Levites who were musicians—Asaph, Heman, Jeduthun, and all their sons and brothers— were dressed in fine linen robes and stood at the east side of the altar playing cymbals, lyres, and harps. They were joined by 120 priests who were playing trumpets.* **13** *The trumpeters and singers performed together in unison to praise and give thanks to the Lord. Accompanied by trumpets, cymbals, and other instruments, they raised their voices and praised the Lord with these words: "He is good! His faithful love endures forever!" At that moment a thick cloud filled the Temple of the Lord.* **14** *The priests could*

> *not continue their service because of the cloud, for the glorious presence of the Lord filled the Temple of God.* (NLT)

Another instance of the power of being united in heart and purpose is seen in the book of Acts, chapter 2, when they were all *"with one accord in one place"*:

> **1** *When the Day of Pentecost had fully come, they were all with one accord in one place.* **2** *And suddenly there came a sound from heaven, as of a rushing mighty wind, and it filled the whole house where they were sitting.* **3** *Then there appeared to them divided tongues, as of fire, and one sat upon each of them.* **4** *And they were all filled with the Holy Spirit and began to speak with other tongues, as the Spirit gave them utterance.* (NKJV)

And the book of Acts, chapter 4, gives another powerful example of the effects of united prayer as they *"raised their voices in unity and prayed"* in response to the persecution of Peter and John.

> **24** *When the believers heard their report, they raised their voices in unity and prayed, "Lord Yahweh, you are the Lord of all! You created the universe—the earth, the sky, the sea, and everything that is in them.* **25** *And you spoke by the Holy Spirit through your servant David, our forefather, saying: 'How dare the nations plan a rebellion, ranting and raging against the Lord Most High? Their foolish plots are futile!* **26** *Look at how the kings of the earth take their stand, with the rulers scheming and conspiring*

together against God[c] and his anointed Messiah!' **27** *"In fact, Herod and Pontius Pilate, along with Jews and non-Jews, met together to take their stand against your holy servant, Jesus the Messiah.* **28** *They did to him all that your purpose and will had determined, according to the destiny you had marked out for him.* **29** *So now, Lord, listen to their threats to harm us. Empower us, as your servants, to speak the word of God freely and courageously.* **30** *Stretch out your hand of power through us to heal, and to move in signs and wonders by the name of your holy Son, Jesus!"* **31** *At that moment the earth shook beneath them, causing the building they were in to tremble. Each one of them was filled with the Holy Spirit, and they proclaimed the word of God with unrestrained boldness.*

One heart, one mind, one accord, lifting up one voice, is the way God has designed things. He made your purpose to work in cooperation with others, especially with the leaders God has placed in your life. Why? Because it all accomplishes the same thing: people knowing and loving God. Your purpose is not independent from the rest of the body unless it is not a part of the body.

So, we cannot say, "I can't see the fulfillment of my dream because no one supports me or because I've experienced resistance." Jesus is the source of our fulfillment; and because His plan for our lives is His idea, He is invested in seeing it come to completion. He wants you to be a part of something bigger than yourself, and He loves your individuality. He loves and likes mankind, and He loves every individual.

GOD'S HOUSE

There is a passage in the Gospel of Mark, chapter 11, that talks about God's house:

> **15** *When they came into Jerusalem, Jesus went directly into the temple area and overturned all the tables and benches of the merchants who were doing business there. One by one he drove them all out of the temple courts, and they scattered away, including the money changers and those selling doves.* **16** *And he would not allow them to use the temple courts as a thoroughfare for carrying their merchandise and their furniture.* **17** *Then he began to teach the people, saying, "Does not the Scripture say, 'My house will be a house of prayer for all the world to share'? But you have made it a thieves' hangout!"*

The tabernacle and temples that the Lord used as a place for His people to meet with Him were merely a prophetic picture of what was to come: a picture of what would be fulfilled in Jesus, the ultimate tabernacle; and in us, as He is making us to become like Jesus. He fulfills His desire by coming and dwelling in us, making us his "house." The Gospel of John says, in chapter 14, *"...he will make his home in you and will live inside you."*

> **16-17** *And I will ask the Father and he will give you another Savior, the Holy Spirit of Truth, who will be to you a friend just like me—and he will never leave you. The world won't receive him because they can't see him or know him. But you will know him intimately, because he will make his home in you and will live inside you.*

And in the First Epistle to the Corinthians, chapter 6, we are called "*the temple of the Holy Spirit:*"

> **19** *Don't you realize that your body is the temple of the Holy Spirit, who lives in you and was given to you by God?* (NLT)

His desire is that we be one with Him as Jesus and the Father are one. This is what Jesus prayed in the Gospel of John, chapter 17:

> **21** *I pray for them all to be joined together as one even as you and I, Father, are joined together as one. I pray for them to become one with us so that the world will recognize that you sent me.*

Jesus states in the passage from the Gospel of Mark, chapter 11, that it had been written in scripture, which is the Word of God, that His Father's house shall be called the house of prayer. This is God's intent for His house. The house where Jesus was at the time—the Temple—was being made a den of thieves, something far less than what God's original purpose for it was. Jesus was jealous over God's original intent for this house, so much so that He dealt with the obstacles to God's purpose for that house. Given how strongly Jesus felt about anything obstructing the purpose of the Temple as His house, and recognizing that this is a prophetic picture of *us* as God's house, we can see how meaningful it is in the heart of God to dwell among men and to fulfill what He has purposed over us.

God wants to be with us. He is jealous over being with us and deals with the enemies of that connection. He is also jealous over God's purpose for us, just as he was jealous over God's purpose for the Temple. They were making the Temple a den of thieves. It had been hundreds of years since the original verse that Jesus referred to, related to this house being 'a house of prayer for all the world to share', was written. In other words, Jesus said, *"I have been waiting more years that you know for the fulfillment of what my purpose is, and I won't let this menial desire of monetary gain be a deterrent."* Similarly, I believe this is also the way God deals with things in us where there are issues that can be a distraction from what He has intended for us. We can let things distract us that are so menial in comparison to what God has for us, and so God allows those things to be exposed for what they really are.

Fun and games in Thika, Kenya.

CHAPTER 16
Making God's Dream Our Dream

God's dream for us is the thing that we really want. Sometimes we recognize it, and sometimes it takes some convincing. God often puts a passion in us for something that is ultimately His will for us. I like how He did it with Luke. It says at the beginning of the Gospel of Luke:

> **1-4** *I am writing for you, mighty lover of God, an orderly account of what Jesus, the Anointed One, accomplished and fulfilled among us. Several eye-witness biographies have already been written, using as their source material the good news preached among us by his early disciples, who became loving servants of the Living Expression. But now I am passing on to you this accurate compilation of my own meticulous investigation based on numerous eyewitness interviews and thorough research of the story of his life. It is appropriate for me to write this,*

*for he also appeared to me so that I would reassure
you beyond any shadow of a doubt the reliability of
all you have been taught of him.*

Luke states in this passage that, because so many had decided to write about the things that they, including him, had experienced while Jesus lived with them in His earthly life, it *"is appropriate,"* seems like the right thing to do. *Sure. Why not, Luke? What can it hurt?* Now as we read the book of Luke, we can see that God was behind that thought and used it as a means to communicate His Word to people for generations—all over the world.

It seemed like a good idea. What might the good ideas you have been destined to do? I believe we'll find our Father inspiring some of those ideas and that we will see Him back them in a way we could never have imagined. It's so worth it to go for it. What if we miss it? Well, the disciples missed it a lot; and I believe those times are recorded in scripture to encourage us to continue, regardless. It was a part of their learning journey as they walked with the Lord, and who are we to believe we're going to get it all without mistakes?

Peter resisted Jesus going to the cross. The disciples didn't want children brought to Jesus. Two of them wanted fire called down on a town that didn't receive Jesus. Peter cut off the ear of one of those who came to arrest Jesus. Those Jesus wanted to pray with Him in His most challenging hour fell asleep, and so on. They didn't get it all right in every situation, and it will be the same for us. They learned, and we're learning. Jesus was not disheartened by their messes, and He isn't and won't be by ours. He knew what He had purposed for them, and He would be the one to bring it to pass. It is the same with us. We can rest assured He is able. One of the things I love, that the Lord says in His word about His purpose over us, is in the Epistle to the Philippians, chapter 2. It says:

> **13** *God will continually revitalize you, implanting within you the passion to do what pleases him.*

It is God working in us for "*what pleases Him.*" In other words, He likes to work in you to do what He's called you to do. It's not a distant kind of "get it done". No, it's "come on, let's do this thing together because this is what I like." God likes the journey of fulfilling what He has purposed over you.

Friend, God has good things for you. There is a false concept of God that makes Him out to be a stoic, kind of unhappy taskmaster, who only wants us to bear down and suffer through our lives until the end. This is not God. I want to look at a biblical picture of our Father for a moment. He has good things for us. Sometimes, I dare say, when we see Him in this negative, stoic way, we are prevented from receiving all the good that He has. This is demonstrated in a parable Jesus told in the Gospel of Luke, chapter 19. It says:

> **11** *At this time Jesus was getting close to entering Jerusalem. The crowds that followed him were convinced that God's kingdom realm would fully manifest when Jesus established it in Jerusalem.* **12** *So he told them this story to change their perspective: "Once there was a wealthy prince who left his province to travel to a distant land, where he would be crowned king and then return.* **13** *Before he departed he summoned his ten servants together and said, 'I am entrusting each of you with fifty thousand dollars*

to trade with while I am away. Invest it and put the money to work until I return.' **14** "Some of his countrymen despised the prince and sent a delegation after him to declare before the royals, 'We refuse to let this man rule over us! He will not be our king!' **15** "Nevertheless, he was crowned king and returned to his land. Then he summoned his ten servants to see how much each one had earned and what their profits came to. **16** "The first one came forward and said, 'Master, I took what you gave me and invested it, and it multiplied ten times.' **17** "'Splendid! You have done well, my excellent servant. Because you have shown that you can be trusted in this small matter, I now grant you authority to rule over ten fortress cities.' **18** "The second came and said, 'Master, what you left with me has multiplied five times.' **19** "His master said, 'I also grant you authority in my kingdom over five fortress cities.' **20** "Another came before the king and said, 'Master, here is the money you entrusted to me. I hid it for safekeeping. **21** You see, I live in fear of you, for everyone knows you are a strict master and impossible to please. You push us for a high return on all that you own, and you always want to gain from someone else's efforts.' **22** "The king said, 'You wicked servant! I will judge you using your own words. If what you said about me is true, that I am a harsh man, pushing you for a high return and wanting gain from others' efforts, **23** why didn't you at least put my money in the bank to earn some interest on what I entrusted to you?' **24** "The king said to his other servants,

'Take the money he has and give it to the faithful servant who multiplied my money ten times over.' **25** *"But master,' the other servants objected, 'why give it to him? He already has so much!' 26 "'Yes,'* *replied the king. 'But to all who have been faithful, even more will be given them. And for the ones who have nothing, even the little they seem to have will be taken from them.*

This passage says, in verse 15, that the master came back to see *how much* every man had gained by trading. It does not say he came to see whether or not they had gained by trading. Why? Because He had a positive outlook related to these men. He was thinking good thoughts toward them. So, God is thinking good thoughts toward us:

> **Jeremiah 29:11** *For I know the plans I have for you," says the Lord. "They are plans for good and not for disaster, to give you a future and a hope.* (NLT)

His expectations were good. The above passage from the Gospel of Luke also says, in verse 15, that He came to see how much *every* man had gained by trading. In other words, He believed in all of them. Not just some, but each and every one. I tell you God has the same thoughts toward us: that He is our biggest fan, if you will, in our corner, cheering us on. He knows what He has made us capable of and is our greatest advocate. He wants to see it all happen in our lives.

The story focuses in on the one who was given money, but who chose not to do anything with it. Let's look at what was going on in the mind of this one. This servant states to the master in verses 20 and 21, *"You push us for a high return on all that*

you own, and you always want to gain from someone else's efforts."
Master you're all about taking. We know this is a false picture
of who this master was. His response to those who had traded
wasn't of taking. It was actually of giving; and not just giving,
but extravagant giving.

When the master interacted with His servants who properly
stewarded their resources, His posture wasn't to consume all that
they had; but His response was to give them even more. You see,
the Lord cares about our character. He doesn't want to just give
us abundance if we aren't even able to handle the little that He
sometimes gives us. He wants us to learn along the way; and this
is for our good, that we might succeed with greater and greater.

My seven-year-old daughter is one of the greatest lovers of
animals there is or has ever been. I'm convinced this kind of love
only comes from God himself. In fact, God does care for animals.
They are His idea. God gave Adam the responsibility of naming
the animals. Anyhow, my daughter loves them a lot. She has
been asking my wife and me for a puppy for a long time. There
is nothing I want more than to see the joy she would get out
of bringing home a new puppy and adding it to her collection
of animals. A closet full of stuffed ones, though, the ones she
already owns, require no care. She will need to learn how to take
care of a real puppy. So, we didn't start her off with one. That is
a leap into responsibility that she has not yet been exposed to.

We decided to start her with a hamster. Mr. Squeaker is his
name. We wanted to see how she does with him—cleaning his
cage, changing his water, showing him love, etc. She's learning
and doing a great job, by the way. And she will get her puppy.

Now, if I care about her success, I'm going to let her learn
and not immediately throw her into full time responsibility for
a puppy. Why? Because she has no experience at it. I want her to

be well equipped so that she can get the joy out of owning one rather than it being an all-consuming burden. I say this because, biblically, I believe God works with us in a similar fashion. It says in the Gospel of Luke, chapter 19:

> **17** *"'Splendid! You have done well, my excellent servant. Because you have shown that you can be trusted in this small matter, I now grant you authority to rule over ten fortress cities.'*

His faithfulness with a little led him into being responsible for more. I would venture to say, also, that this was always a part of the master's plan. I say this because this parable is a picture of God and His children. And as it says in the verse above, from the book Jeremiah, His good thoughts have to do with getting us to an expected end. He is not making it up as we go along but has the whole thing planned out as He leads us through to fulfillment of His purposes.

Again, it says in the Gospel of Luke, chapter 19, verse 17, "… I now grant you authority to rule over ten fortress cities." How does one go from being faithful over a pound to being in authority to rule over ten fortress cities? Simply put, that is our God. And that is why we can dream, because not only can He do *"…exceeding abundantly above all we ask or think,"* as we are told in the Epistle to the Ephesians, chapter 3, verse 20 (KJV), but He wants us to know it well. He wants us to know that even our dreams cannot exceed the good that He has for us. The Passion Translation, says it this way:

> **Ephesians 3:20** *Never doubt God's mighty power to work in you and accomplish all this. He will achieve infinitely more than your greatest request, your most*

> *unbelievable dream, and exceed your wildest imag-*
> *ination! He will outdo them all, for his miraculous*
> *power constantly energizes you.*

He isn't as the last servant in the parable saw Him, austere
and selfish. That was a false concept, meant to represent how
some misinterpret God. But our God is neither austere nor
selfish. He is good. Psalm 34 gives us one of many statements
of His goodness:

> **8** *O taste and see that the Lord is good: blessed is*
> *the man that trusteth in him.* (KJV)

This servant's incorrect estimation of his master kept him
from experiencing all that the master had for him. The Passion
Translation states this verse in Psalm 34 a little differently:

> **8** *Drink deeply of the pleasures of this God. Expe-*
> *rience for yourself the joyous mercies he gives to all*
> *who turn to hide themselves in him.*

"Experience for yourself the joyous mercies he gives to all who
turn to hide themselves in him." How do we do that? Just as in
any relationship, we get to know the character of another by
being with them. The more you are with a person, the more
you know them. The Lord says in this word that, in being with
Him, goodness is what you can look forward to. Does that mean
everything is going to go perfectly the way you want it in your
life? No. But it does mean that in times of challenge, you can
expect His goodness. As it says in the Epistle to the Romans,
chapter 8:

> **28** *So we are convinced that every detail of our lives*

is continually woven together to fit into God's perfect plan of bringing good into our lives, for we are his lovers who have been called to fulfill his designed purpose.

You can't get away from His goodness. David said in Psalm 23:

6 *So why would I fear the future? For your goodness and love pursue me all the days of my life. Then afterward, when my life is through, I'll return to your glorious presence to be forever with you!*

Part of the definition of the word 'pursue' here means that His goodness will harass you and chase you down. I have experienced times in my life when I had to say, *"No, God, you can't be this good."* There have been times when I felt like I had made some of the worst decisions out of anger or frustration, but those were the times when He showed up and demonstrated His goodness the most. I believe, from experience and from scripture, that no matter where we are, no matter what we've done, we can still expect the goodness of God in our lives. He is always good. That is His character. Our view of Him doesn't change that fact. But our view of Him can affect what we allow ourselves to experience with Him.

He says "taste," and that means to be with him, to enjoy Him. We don't have to stay in a place of not seeing how good He is; we can be with him and have a real taste of that goodness.

Celebrating our new home in Kinshasa.

CHAPTER 17

Closer and Closer to Him

Luke 4:14 *Then Jesus, armed with the Holy Spirit's power, returned to Galilee, and his fame spread throughout the region.* **15** *He taught in the synagogues and they glorified him.* **16-17** *When he came to Nazareth, where he had been raised, he went into the synagogue, as he always did on the Sabbath day. When Jesus came to the front to read the Scriptures, they handed him the scroll of the prophet Isaiah. He unrolled the scroll and read where it is written,* **18-19** *"The Spirit of the Lord is upon me, and he has anointed me to be hope for the poor, freedom for the brokenhearted, and new eyes for the blind, and to preach to prisoners, 'You are set free!' I have come to share the message of Jubilee, for the time of God's great acceptance has begun."* **20** *After he read this he rolled up the scroll, handed it back to the minister, and sat down. Everyone stared at Jesus,* *wondering what he was about to say.* **21** *Then he added, "These Scriptures came true today in front of you."* **22** *Everyone was impressed by how well Jesus spoke, in awe of the beautiful words of grace that came from his lips. But they were surprised at his presumption to speak as a prophet, so they said among themselves, "Who does he think he is? This is Joseph's son, who grew up here in Nazareth."* **23** *Jesus said to them, "I suppose you'll quote me the proverb, 'Doctor, go and heal yourself before you try to heal others.' And you'll say, 'Work the miracles here in your hometown that we heard you did in Capernaum.'* **24** *But let me tell you, no prophet is welcomed or honored in his own hometown.* **25** *"Isn't it true that there were many widows in the land of Israel during the days of the prophet Elijah when he locked up the heavens for three and a half years and brought a devastating famine over all the land?* **26** *But he wasn't sent to any of the widows living in that region. Instead, he was sent to a foreign place, to a widow in Zarephath of Sidon.* **27** *Or have you not considered that the prophet Elisha healed only Naaman, the Syrian, rather than one of the many Jewish lepers living in the land?"* **28** *When everyone present heard those words, they erupted with furious rage.* **29** *They mobbed Jesus and threw him out of the city, dragging him to the edge of the cliff on the hill on which the city had been built, ready to hurl him off.* **30** *But he walked right through the crowd, leaving them all stunned.* **31** *Jesus went to Capernaum in Galilee and taught the people on* *the Sabbath day.* **32** *His teachings stunned and dazed them, for he spoke with penetrating words that manifested great authority.*

We see by looking at the above passage, that Jesus had come home to the town He was raised in; and there He went to the synagogue, as was His custom. However, there was something unique about this particular visit to the synagogue. It says in verse 22 that *"Everyone was impressed by how well Jesus spoke, in awe of the beautiful words of grace that came from his lips."* There was something about His words this time that captured them.

Whenever God begins to demonstrate who He is, we are presented with an invitation. That is what was happening there. Jesus was giving those in the synagogue an opportunity – or an invitation—to see who He was on an unusual level; one they were not accustomed to. And they immediately began to draw from what their experience had been with Him. Basically, they realized they had never seen Him like this before; and they didn't know how to relate to Him except to lean on, or try to draw from, what they had seen before. To them, He was Joseph's son, the brother of the family they were so familiar with. When He revealed Himself in a new way, they couldn't get beyond the familiar.

That is something that we face as well, because when we walk with Him, Jesus is constantly drawing us into a greater depth of intimacy with Him, revealing more of Himself to us. There are things about Him we have yet to experience, and we will do ourselves a favor to accept the invitation to know Him more. This is a real challenge to our natural man because, when we see Him in a new way, we're also seeing what *we* are called to be – in a new way. That moment when we see, we have the opportunity to embrace the change that He is inviting us into—that He may have a bride, a companion, that is mutual in her character.

On the other hand, we can choose to dig our heels in and stay where we are. That is what was done by those in that synagogue on that day. He said to them in verse 24 that *"no prophet is welcomed or honored in his own hometown."* He went on to say in verses 25- 26 that there were many widows in the days of Elijah, when great famine was in the land, but *"he wasn't sent to any of the widows living in that region. Instead, he was sent to a foreign place, to a widow in Zarephath of Sidon."* This was a woman who was outside of the commonwealth of Israel. Jesus was saying that it was God's desire to send Elijah to many of the widows in the country of His covenant people. In other words, there were things available in that day that were missed by those who could have accessed them. If not for the lack of acceptance of Elijah being a sent one of God, many more could have been blessed.

There are things that God intends for us to lay hold of that are available to us in our day, things that may not be what we've experienced: breakthroughs, if we are willing. Will we accept what He wants to show us of Himself, even if we may not have seen it before?

In this regard, I think we should also look more closely at one of the passages Jesus refers to. It says in the book of 1 Kings, chapter 17:

> **1** *Now Elijah, who was from Tishbe in Gilead, told King Ahab, "As surely as the Lord, the God of Israel, lives—the God I serve—there will be no dew or rain during the next few years until I give the word!"* **2** *Then the Lord said to Elijah,* **3** *"Go to the east and hide by Kerith Brook, near where it enters*

the Jordan River. **4** *Drink from the brook and eat what the ravens bring you, for I have commanded them to bring you food."* **5** *So Elijah did as the Lord told him and camped beside Kerith Brook, east of the Jordan.* **6** *The ravens brought him bread and meat each morning and evening, and he drank from the brook.* **7** *But after a while the brook dried up, for there was no rainfall anywhere in the land.* **8** *Then the Lord said to Elijah,* **9** *"Go and live in the village of Zarephath, near the city of Sidon. I have instructed a widow there to feed you."* **10** *So he went to Zarephath. As he arrived at the gates of the village, he saw a widow gathering sticks, and he asked her, "Would you please bring me a little water in a cup?"* **11** *As she was going to get it, he called to her, "Bring me a bite of bread, too."* **12** *But she said, "I swear by the Lord your God that I don't have a single piece of bread in the house. And I have only a handful of flour left in the jar and a little cooking oil in the bottom of the jug. I was just gathering a few sticks to cook this last meal, and then my son and I will die."* **13** *But Elijah said to her, "Don't be afraid! Go ahead and do just what you've said, but make a little bread for me first. Then use what's left to prepare a meal for yourself and your son.* **14** *For this is what the Lord, the God of Israel, says: There will always be flour and olive oil left in your containers until the time when the Lord sends rain and the crops grow again!"* **15** *So she did as Elijah said, and she and Elijah and her family continued to eat for many days.* **16** *There was always enough* *flour and olive oil left in the containers, just as the Lord had promised through Elijah.* (NLT)

Verse 16 says *"…just as the Lord had promised through Elijah."* What are you hearing in a time when everything looks negative?

Birds don't bake bread. Where do birds get enough bread to feed a man? And where on earth did they get meat? This was something completely supernatural. I would not be surprised if they brought him a whole loaf wrapped up hot and ready, buttered and all. That is why it was so easy for Elijah to believe for the widow to be sustained—because he had just come out of living in that same place. He'd come from having nothing, and then having it made available supernaturally. And if we are going to be an answer for those who have nothing, we are going to have to believe God when it looks like there is nothing.

WHO ARE YOU IN YOUR GENERATION?

The way we live has an impact on our culture and our generation. The Epistle to the Philippians, chapter 2, says:

> **14** *Live a cheerful life, without complaining or division among yourselves.* **15** *For then you will be seen as innocent, faultless, and pure children of God, even though you live in the midst of a brutal and perverse culture. For you will appear among them as shining lights in the universe,*

And the book of Acts, chapter 13, says in verse 36 that David *"… passionately served God's desires for his generation…."*

Like everyone else, I have a human tendency to want to complain, even though I know better. When problems arise, we have a choice. Widows of Israel in the days of Elijah were many. However, only one of them was available to God to be a testimony of what He was able to do in that situation. To the people in the synagogue to whom Jesus spoke, the reference to there being many widows meant that there were more through whom God wanted to bring a testimony. Only one of them was available to be a testimony: one personal breakthrough where there might have been many.

We are called to a different economy. We have a choice. No matter what is happening in our nation, even if our nation is in wickedness, we are called as God's people to live according to a different economy. We are supposed to be the most hopeful people in the world.

This is why people of God are the real leaders of nations. Can you imagine if the nation of Israel had begun to see people start to receive supernatural provision on a mass scale? Can you imagine how the people would have been touched?

Will you be a leader in your nation?

Think about the response to Jesus in the synagogue. *"Who does he think he is? This is Joseph's son, who grew up here in Nazareth." Aren't things going to continue as they've always been? God does not have anything ready and available to produce as an answer for the situation of our nation. Is it really prophesied? Is it really coming? It's for another day; God is going to, but later."* But what if God is doing something right now? And what if He is inviting you to be a catalyst in it? What answer is He calling you to be in this world?

Tradition says the reason they looked at Jesus the way they did that day was because there was a seat in each synagogue that was reserved for the Messiah, and He took it; and that action was so out-of-the-box that it drew a marked level of attention. The Bible doesn't say that. It says that they were "…impressed by how well Jesus spoke, in awe of the beautiful words of grace that came from his lips." Because of this, I submit to you that their amazed response was in direct relationship to the supernatural power that was on the words that He was speaking. I also recognize that we often do the same thing they did in this passage, in response to the unusual: we try to explain away supernatural things when God brings them.

Later in the Gospel of Luke, chapter 4, verses 32 and 36, say that they glorified Him because of His word—because His word was with power.

> **32** *And they were astonished at his doctrine: for his word was with power.... * **36** *And they were all amazed, and spake among themselves, saying, What a word is this! for with authority and power he commandeth the unclean spirits, and they come out.* (KJV)

It had to do with the power of the word. We sometimes want to water it down to some natural thing. I've heard it said by some that the Red Sea opened by a naturally explained means when Moses was leading the children of Israel out of Egypt. But those who say such things can't explain the supernatural nature of the timing in which it happened.

We have to dream. Dreaming is not some lofty thing. It is basically agreeing with what God says about us. I will finish with this story, again of John the Baptist. In the Gospel of Matthew, in chapter 11, it says of John the Baptist:

> **2** *John the Baptist, who was in prison, heard about all the things the Messiah was doing. So he sent his disciples to ask Jesus,* **3** *"Are you the Messiah we've been expecting, or should we keep looking for someone*

else?" 4 Jesus told them, "Go back to John and tell him what you have heard and seen—5 the blind see, the lame walk, those with leprosy are cured, the deaf hear, the dead are raised to life, and the Good News is being preached to the poor." 6 And he added, "God blesses those who do not fall away because of me." 7 As John's disciples were leaving, Jesus began talking about him to the crowds. "What kind of man did you go into the wilderness to see? Was he a weak reed, swayed by every breath of wind? 8 Or were you expecting to see a man dressed in expensive clothes? No, people with expensive clothes live in palaces. 9 Were you looking for a prophet? Yes, and he is more than a prophet. 10 John is the man to whom the Scriptures refer when they say, 'Look, I am sending my messenger ahead of you, and he will prepare your way before you.' 11 "I tell you the truth, of all who have ever lived, none is greater than John the Baptist. Yet even the least person in the Kingdom of Heaven is greater than he is! (NLT)

So, Jesus responded to John with a confirmation of who He was, not by a convincing word only, but by the testimony of the things His own disciples had witnessed. When John's disciples left Jesus in order to answer John, Jesus turned to the people around Him and asked who they went out to see when they went to see John. He gave them a few options to respond with, and then told them who it was they went to see.

I love what Jesus said here because John was then probably at his personal lowest, needing confirmation, and perhaps questioning what He was once so confident of. He needed his mission confirmed. He had introduced Jesus to the nation with a confident decree, as stated in the Gospel of John, chapter 1, verse 29 (NKJV): *"Behold! The Lamb of God who takes away the sin of the world!"* And he wanted to be sure he had finished well. Not only did Jesus confirm John, he declared to the crowd where He was ministering that there had not been a greater prophet in history.

Friends, no matter how you feel, no matter whether you feel you've messed up or don't qualify for your dream, God still has great things to say about you. He is in your corner, cheering you on.

So go ahead, feed the five thousand men plus women and children, forgetting that you only have five loaves and two fish with which to do it. Heal the sick, cleanse the leper, raise the dead, cast out devils. None of these things can be done without Him. However, He is so committed to being with you, that when He calls us to participate in something of kingdom advancement, He doesn't consider a thought of us not being vitally connected to Him. With God, all things are possible. All things that He has invited us to participate with Him in, by being intimately connected to Him, we will see impossibilities bow to the name of Jesus.

What does that look like? The Lord Jesus telling our team He wanted to heal during a service when we were ministering. It looks like a woman named Roberta. Roberta had been diagnosed with breast cancer and had surgery, which addressed the illness at the time. However, a couple of years later, she was found to have end-stage cancer which had spread aggressively with generalized metastasis in her bones, ribs, lungs and intestines. She also had a tumor on her brain. She was in constant pain, and the doctors said they had done all they could, as she was too weak to withstand any more of the side effects of the chemo. Roberta was invited to join the service on the night that our team was ministering at the Iris Ministry Base. She came to the service. Before the team leader preached, he began to pray, and shared that he felt an anointing for healing was in that place. He specifically called out cancer and prayed for healing of cancer before starting to preach.

At that moment, Roberta felt like God was operating on her. She felt a fire burning inside of her, like a river of fire of God's healing. For the next three days, she felt a burning in her body. On the third day she had a routine scan that had been previously scheduled, and the scan showed that she was totally healed! Not only had all the metastatic growths gone but also her brain tumor had vanished, and to top it all off the doctor was shocked as she had been given new blood and it was discovered that her own blood type had changed from B to AB negative. She told of details such as name of doctors and etc.

She gives all honor and glory to Jesus!

I would like to say that a member of our team contacted this woman to confirm details and glorify God with this victory. She authorized the story to be told of this amazing wonder of God.

Before this miracle, I had never heard of anyone's blood type being changed. It's interesting because I worked in a lab where blood was processed in a medical facility, and anyone who knows how that process works knows that blood that is donated to another person has to be "typed and cross-matched." That means that anyone receiving blood from a donation must receive one of two types: either type O, which is the only universal type and can be donated to anyone of any blood type, or the recipient's own blood type. Any other combination will cause a fatality. I know this from working in the medical field. I believe that part of this miracle in the testimony above was the signature of God showing that He, and He alone, healed this lady. We believe in the blessing that the Lord has provided through the medical community, but God can do exceedingly abundantly above anything that we can think or imagine.

Having said that, I want to encourage you to dream, and dream again! What God has called you to do seems impossible because it's supposed to be impossible, but He has never called you to do anything that is independent of Him. His heart has been, and will always be, that you and He be one as He prayed in the Gospel of John chapter seventeen. You are such a gift to this generation, and you have so much to give. The world needs what you have. Let the blessing that you are continue to give the people around you a glimpse of how much Jesus loves them, because He extends His love to them through you. Keep your passion for Him burning. God bless you. We are waiting for you.

ABOUT THE AUTHOR

Kevin and Robin Shipp, founders of Desire of Nations, a ministry focusing communicating the love of Jesus Christ and helping disadvantaged children. The Shipps have been involved in lay ministry for 20 years. Kevin is an ordained Assemblies of God minister and Robin is credentialed teacher. They have two children who also serve as a part of Desire of Nations.

All proceeds from the sale of this book will go towards the ministry work of Desire of Nations
Visit our website to find out more:
https://desireofnations.net/How-to-Help

Made in the USA
Columbia, SC
30 January 2022